Documenting Psychotherapy

Documenting Psychotherapy

Essentials for Mental Health Practitioners

Mary E. Moline
George T. Williams
Kenneth M. Austin

 SAGE Publications
International Educational and Professional Publisher
Thousand Oaks   London   New Delhi

For information:

 SAGE Publications, Inc.
2455 Teller Road
Thousand Oaks, California 91320
E-mail: order@sagepub.com

SAGE Publications Ltd.
6 Bonhill Street
London EC2A 4PU
United Kingdom

SAGE Publications India Pvt. Ltd.
M-32 Market
Greater Kailash I
New Delhi 110 048 India

Printed in the United States of America

Library of Congress Cataloging-in-Publication Data

Moline, Mary E.
    Documenting psychotherapy: Essentials for mental health practitioners
by Mary E. Moline, George T. Williams, Kenneth M. Austin
        p. cm.
    Includes bibliographical references and index.
    ISBN 0-8039-4691-0 (cloth: acid-free paper).—ISBN 0-8039-4692-9
(pbk.: acid-free paper)
    1. Psychiatric records. I. Williams, George Taylor. II. Austin,
Kenneth M. III. Title.
RC455.2.M38M65   199797-4884
651.5'04261—dc21

98 99 00 01 02 03 04 10 9 8 7 6 5 4 3 2

Acquiring Editor:	Jim Nageotte
Editorial Assistant:	Kathleen Derby
Production Editor:	Sanford Robinson
Production Assistant:	Denise Santoyo
Copy Editor:	Joyce Kuhn
Typesetter/Designer:	Marion S. Warren
Indexer:	Molly Hall
Cover Designer:	Anahid Moradkhan
Print Buyer:	Anna Chin

Contents

Preface

Each of us has contributed equally to the writing of this book, so there is no senior author. Although we had responsibilities for certain chapters, we collaborated in revising the contents into the final form.

When we first became aware of the various issues involved in keeping psychotherapeutic records, we were researching court cases for our first book, *Confronting Malpractice: Legal and Ethical Dilemmas in Psychotherapy* (1990). It was conspicuous that psychotherapists were not brought to court because of improper records but, rather, that their defense was weakened because of poor, or lack of, record keeping. Therefore, we became interested in researching various aspects of record keeping and formulated questions to investigate: Is there genuinely a need for good records? Are there laws regarding record keeping? What do our colleagues believe regarding records? Do records serve both the client and the therapist equally? What do related professional organizations advise about keeping records? What comprises a "good record"? When issues of confidentiality (e.g., harm to self or others) become apparent, how should one record them? Are there any requirements for storing and destroying records? Our interest in answering these and other frequently asked questions became the motivation factor for writing this book.

We maintain that inadequate record keeping or having no record can negatively affect the outcome of a case against a psychotherapist. On August 21, 1994, *Los Angeles Times Magazine* indicated that there are 8,000 to 10,000 lawsuits against psychotherapists pending in United States courts, and at least 1,000 of them are in California. We only hope that all of these psychotherapists have kept good records.

Because of the litigious nature of contemporary America, it is vital that both licensed psychotherapists and students in the field of mental health learn how to keep good records. We are not members of the legal profession, so our comments and evaluations of legal cases are presented from the perspective of mental health professionals. Please note that the implications of these cases will differ from state to state. If you need more information, check with an attorney, your state licensing board, or your professional association.

Keeping good records is not just a method to avoid litigation. We firmly believe that good record keeping supports the therapist in conducting professional duties and thus assists in providing appropriate care for clients. This consideration, we believe, outweighs any legal deliberation.

We have divided this book into five parts. At the beginning of each part, the contents of its chapters are briefly discussed. The structure for all chapters is to follow the presentation of the material with a brief summary. Throughout this book, we refer to California laws because it would have been too cumbersome a task to include the relevant laws for all states in the nation. One or more court cases are presented to give the reader an illustration of legal decisions as well as similarities and differences between the states. Some questions follow the court cases. These questions were designed to stimulate thought. Some have several possible answers. After the questions, one or more vignettes are presented. Again, there may be more than one solution to a vignette. Appendix K presents one possible answer to one vignette in each chapter.

Acknowledgments

This book took a good deal of our time and coordinated effort. We wish to thank our families for their support and encouragement.

PART I

THE IMPORTANCE OF RECORD KEEPING IN PSYCHOTHERAPY

*T*his section is divided into two chapters. Chapter 1 covers therapist attitudes about record keeping and protecting both the client and the therapist. Chapter 2 focuses on the limits of confidentiality and mandatory reporting.

CHAPTER 1

Protecting the Client and the Therapist

Record keeping has become an imperative in clinical work. This chapter emphasizes that keeping records is significant not only for the therapist, but the client as well. The significance of keeping records has both ethical and legal considerations. The legal considerations become paramount when the clinician's records are subpoenaed, and in this chapter we discuss some helpful hints on how to deal with a subpoena. We will conclude with relevant legal cases, vignettes, and questions to further stimulate your thinking. We do not answer questions posed, for our intent was to take you beyond the boundaries of each chapter. If you find that you do not have answers, we hope you will discuss the questions with colleagues, professors, and fellow students.

Do you keep records on each of your clients? Are you confused about what you need to write down in your client's records? Could the following case represent you if your records were subpoenaed?

You have been seeing a client for over a year. You have helped her overcome a suicidal period, work through her issues of abuse,

3

and become a better parent. You also helped her decide to leave a relationship (an extramarital affair) she had for the past year. You did not treat her husband nor her children. In addition, your record keeping was brief and somewhat sloppy. You were not sure how to organize your thoughts and actions but that did not concern you until you received a subpoena for her records. The subpoena was submitted on her husband's behalf. He is currently requesting a divorce. He wishes to prove that his wife is an unfit mother so he can obtain custody of their children.

What do you do? How do you evaluate your method of keeping records? Do you erase any of what you wrote down or add to it? Do you notify your client that you have been issued a subpoena for her records? Do you feel somewhat embarrassed as to how you kept records and wonder how the legal system might interpret them? Are you concerned about the manner in which you addressed her issues of suicide, abuse, and the affair? Do you have any idea what to do once you have been subpoenaed? If these are questions you would like to have answered, you will find this book an appropriate resource.

We hope to increase your awareness of how your record-keeping procedures can determine the outcome of a legal case brought against you. Although such a case is not likely to be due to inadequate record keeping, such practice could negatively affect the outcome of your case. Some therapists view it as unwise to keep detailed records about their clients. However, if you become involved in a lawsuit, you are likely to be deemed as behaving unprofessionally if you have not kept adequate records (Austin, Moline, & Williams, 1990).

Attitudes About Record Keeping

Before writing the book, we asked therapists what they thought was the significance of keeping records. Moreover, we asked if they believed it was important to keep records. Persons informally surveyed suggested two main rationales for *not* maintaining any client records: It is a method for protecting their clients, and it is a method to protect themselves against ligitation. We were fascinated to learn of their decision, as various professional associations advise psychotherapists to keep records, and there has been a sharp increase in malpractice suits. Even with the number of complaints from licensing boards and ethics committees on the rise, respondents nonetheless argued against keeping records.

Arguments Against

Although controversy exists among some mental health professionals about keeping records in psychotherapy, we have been unable to find any written commentary against keeping written records. Arguments presented here are largely taken from verbal comments related by various psychotherapists too numerous to credit or who are reluctant to be identified as being opposed to record keeping. The reasons given for not keeping records are listed in Table 1.1.

Arguments For

The reasons for good record keeping in psychotherapy are numerous. Table 1.2 lists some of the major reasons we have discovered, not only in our own practices but in reading and researching various resources, that record keeping is good practice.

Protecting the Client

The most common explanation for not keeping records is from therapists who feel keeping records *breaches client confidentiality and privileged communication.* These therapists may have good intentions, but they are also operating on the faulty premise that clients cannot protect themselves. Clients have certain rights which protect what they communicate to their therapists. Their records cannot be shared unless they waive their rights and give permission for records to be viewed by outside resources or a release is ordered by a judge.

TABLE 1.1 Arguments for Therapists Not Keeping Records

- Therapists believe they can better maintain confidentiality with their clients by not keeping records.
- Some clients request that their therapists keep no records.
- Therapists fear someone (e.g., client, attorney, insurance company) might take issue with what is stated in the record.
- Since it is impossible to write down everything a client says, the therapist who keeps records might have to justify why something from a session *did not* get recorded.
- Some therapists want to keep process notes (e.g., the client's fantasies and feelings; the therapist's reactions and hypotheses formed). They argue that such "working notes" do not belong in a client's record and feel any disclosure (to the client or court) is an invasion of the therapist's privacy.
- Some therapists claim that accurate record keeping is very time consuming.
- No record is better than an inadequate record. Some therapists seem unsure of what is contained in a good record.
- Records are only to protect the therapist in litigation. Since the therapist does not intend to do anything wrong, there is no need to keep records.
- We have heard this message from therapists: "It is in my client's best interest not to keep records."
- One therapist even said that keeping records would make him accountable, and he wasn't going to be accountable to anyone. (We think he forgot about the state board that issued his license.)

Confidentiality can also be protected by consciously being aware of what is written into client records. Act as if others will be reading the records as you write about your client(s). Without being untruthful, write only the critical pieces of information, not words that might be embarrassing. What would you want your clients to observe by reading your account of them?

Record keeping assures your clients that appropriate procedures are being followed. Records are a method by which you can follow the direction of treatment in a meticulous and meaningful manner. If you have a full client case load, you might not remember what various hypotheses were generated and followed, what medication has been prescribed and the amount, or what messages from the client may need follow up, such as discussing sequential depressive episodes.

TABLE 1.2 Arguments for Therapists Keeping Records

- Record keeping is a standard set by many professional organizations in the mental health field (e.g., ACA, APA, AAMFT, and NASW). Thus, failure to keep records is likely to result in working below the "standard of care" in your profession.
- The clinical record can serve as a defense against malpractice claims.
- The clinical record can serve the client by reflecting the client's condition at a specific time. For example, the client might be alleging damage from a recent accident and require the support of your records.
- Records serve the client by documenting that treatment occurred. A client may need such records to validate her court-appointed attendance or to receive reimbursement from her insurance company.
- Records assist in the event that you are unavailable or the client transfers to a new therapist.
- A record can help improve your psychotherapy skills. It is impossible for you to recall all significant material that arises in all of the client's treatment each week. The ability to keep track of your client can assist you in providing appropriate care.
- Records can help in the management of your practice.
- Good records can help protect your license if charges are ever filed against you with the licensing board.
- Good records can assist you if you are charged with an ethical violation.
- Your judgment can be evaluated retrospectively. The record should present evidence of care in judgment.
- Health insurance companies are becoming more aggressive in the area of peer review and increasingly making third-party payments contingent upon retroactive review of the complete record for clients. If records are inadequate or nonexistent, reimbursement may be denied.
- Federal and/or state law may require adequate record keeping.

To protect clients, it has become a "standard of care" practice to address the limits of confidentiality before any therapeutic process begins (see Chapter 2). If you are an intern or a psychological assistant, your supervisor will need to examine each client's record. This too, must be explained before treatment. The client who has signed a consent form to allow the supervisor to observe records needs to discuss what rights have been waived. For example, you must enter into a client's record *any directives given by your supervisor*. Thus, your client will understand that you will not be following your own directives as an unlicensed professional. Furthermore, if you need to assess the direction of a case with your supervisor or obtain a consult from a colleague, you will want to have accurate notes in hand.

Finally, what if you were to move out of state or die? Good records would provide the new therapist in charge the information needed to adequately follow up.

Protecting the Therapist

Properly kept records can favorably influence the outcome of a malpractice suit (*Austin, Moline, & Williams,* 1990; Soisson, VandeCreek, & Knapp, 1987). The courts view *a failure to keep records as a failure to give service.* Many experts (Bennett, Bryant, VandenBos, & Greenwood, 1990; Soisson et al., 1987; Stromberg et al., 1988) relate that clear and concise record keeping is mandatory for successful review by the legal system, insurance companies, and supervisors.

Moreover, your records can help you effectively follow a treatment plan for your client. Records also allow you to recall details. Mentioning the name of a favorite uncle shared ten sessions earlier, for example, makes a client feel respected and heard. The standards set by your professional organization more than likely have a code requiring you to keep records for each client. In California, the legislature asks health care providers to maintain patient records (California Health and Safety Code, 123105, 123115, 123130). Although state laws may vary, it is apparent that most states now require mental health records be kept by the service provider.

Ethical Codes

Standard of Care

To determine if a legal duty by a psychotherapist has been breached, the courts use a yardstick referred to as the "standard of care." The courts usually look to professional standards of ethics to examine how the ordinary and proponent practitioner might act under similar circumstances. This standard of behavior is usually established by the testimony of experts.

Individuals who hold themselves out to the public as expert in some professional area will be held to a higher standard of care, that is, that of a *specialist.* This is true even if the person in question has falsely represented himself as a specialist. Are you aware of what record keeping your professional organizations and licensing boards expect of you as a specialist? What can happen to you if you do not follow their advice?

Guidelines for Professionals

Appendix L provides excerpts from several official codes that have been adopted by different major mental health groups.

The following six professional organizations have representative codes of ethics within a variety of mental health disciplines: (a) the American Psychological Association (APA; 1992), (b) the American Psychiatric Association (AmPsyA; 1989), (c) the American Counseling Association (ACA; 1995), (d) the American Association for Marriage and Family Therapy (AAMFT; 1991), (e) the National Association of Social Workers (NASW; 1996), and (f) the Association for Specialists in Group Work (ASGW; 1989). Four of these (APA, ACA, AAMFT, and NASW) are considered "parent" organizations, while the American Psychiatric Association (AmPsyA here to avoid confusion with APA) is a division of the American Medical Association (AMA), and ASGW is one of the 17 divisions of ACA. It is worthwhile to include ASGW's code because group work is a specialty within the mental health disciplines. APA has several ethical codes, including *Ethical Principles in the Conduct of Research With Human Participants* (1982), *General Guidelines for Providers of Psychological Services* (1987), and, particularly, *Ethical Principles of Psychologists and Code of Conduct* (1992).

Legal Issues

Legislation

Several California laws show the need for mental health professionals to keep accurate and complete records. We refer to

California as an example because we, the three authors of this book, are all California licensed mental health professionals. Legislation in this state took effect on January 1, 1988, for example, that required the Department of Consumer Affairs to develop a brochure to assist victims of psychotherapist/patient sexual abuse.

In early 1990, a brochure titled *Professional Therapy Never Includes Sex* was made available to all licensed psychotherapists (psychologists; psychiatrists; social workers; and marriage, family, and child counselors) in California. The brochure states, under Client Bill of Rights, that a client has the right to request and, in most cases, receive a summary of his file including the diagnosis, the progress, and type of treatment and request the transfer of a copy of this file to any chosen therapist or agency.

In California, it is clear that psychotherapists must keep records. Complete records must be maintained for 7 years.

Subpoenas

Imagine yourself in the following scenario:

You are about to close your office for the weekend when you meet a bike messenger. The messenger gives you an envelope, asks you to sign for it, and rides off. Inside the envelope you find a summons to appear at a hearing and instructions to bring all treatment records you have for a client you had treated two years prior. Your stomach suddenly feels empty, and you go back to your desk and start digging through your files.

What would you do in this situation? Who would you need to consult with? What are you hoping you already had done prior to this occasion?

The most common legal demand of a psychotherapist for information about a client is a subpoena. You might be required to submit a copy of your records or to testify, or both. All that is usually needed to obtain a subpoena is for the attorney to attest that she has reason to believe that you, the psychotherapist, have information relevant to the case.

If your client has not signed a release, you can encourage the client to have his attorney file a motion to "quash" (cancel) the subpoena. Also, you could, at your expense, have legal counsel do the same. Whenever in doubt, check with an attorney after receiving the document. A subpoena can ask for all or specific sections of your client's record believed to be relevant to the case.

It should be noted that section 2.3.7 of the APA's *General Guidelines for Providers of Psychological Services* (1987) states, "Psychological data should be released only to a person recognized by the psychologist as competent to interpret the data, such as test results."

Testing Data/Instruments

The Psychological Corporation's position on copyright infringement opposes the release of copies of the protocols or test and test materials. Their rationale is that this poses a threat to the security and integrity of the materials, thus threatening the validity and value of the measurement instruments. There is less objection to materials being released to persons who are professionals because they are bound by professional ethics not to disclose this information to non-mental-health professionals.

In New Mexico, the presidents of both the state bar and the state psychological association developed a formal statement of principles agreeing that instruments such as the Rorschach, TAT (Thematic Apperception Test) cards, testing materials, and other copyright instruments should be revealed only to qualified psychologists retained by a requesting attorney. Ohio state law agrees with this position.

Title 16 of the California Administrative Code in Section 1396.3 covers test security and states that

a psychologist shall not reproduce or describe in public or in publications subject to general public distribution any psychological tests or other assessment devices, the value of which depends in whole or in part on the naivete of the subject, in ways that might invalidate the techniques; and shall limit access to such tests or devices to persons with professional interests who will safeguard their use.

If Records Are Subpoenaed

We suggest the following guidelines if your records should be subpoenaed:

1. Ask for the requester's identity and verify official capacity.
2. Reasons not to adhere to a request:
   - The information you possess is not relevant to the case.
   - The client did not give consent for release.
   - The law (confidentiality/privilege) protects against the release of your records.
3. Discuss with your client what the implication might be if records were released and how the client will respond.
4. If the client has a legal representative, obtain his or her consent.
5. Remember, the client might read the records.
6. Reasons to adhere to a request for information:
   - A client signed the consent form.
   - A legal representative signed the consent form.
   - The law requires disclosure.
   - Disclosure falls under laws pertaining to harm to self and/or others.
   - The subpoena is valid.
   - If consent is not given, consult the judge or lawyers regarding the law and your own or your client's rights.
   - Document any client communication regarding consent for responding to the subpoena, including whom you consulted, the rationale for disclosure, what information has been released, the date, the time, and the circumstances.
   - Protect confidentiality to the extent allowed by the law.

Summary

In this chapter, arguments for and against record keeping were cited. For the past 20 years, experts have been advising psychotherapists to keep good records, and during the past 10 years, professional ethics codes have promoted the value of records. Record keeping serves both the client and you, the therapist, by demonstrating that treatment occurred and that the evaluation and therapy plan was consistent with the standards of the profession. The courts use professional "standard of care" criteria to determine legal responsibility. Six professional organizations' codes of ethics were examined: the American Psychological Association (APA), the American Psychiatric Association (AmPsyA), the American Counseling Association (ACA), the American Association for Marriage and Family Therapy (AAMFT), the National Association for Social Workers (NASW), and the Association for Specialists in Group Work (ASGW). Examples of relevant legal issues were given, and guidelines to follow when records are subpoenaed were provided. When a conflict exists between a professional ethics code and state law, the state law prevails.

Relevant Court Cases

Victor J. Whitree, Claimant v. State of New York, Defendant
Court of Claims of New York
290 NYS 486 (May 14, 1968)

Inadequate record keeping contributed to the wrongful confinement of a psychiatric patient, Victor J. Whitree, at Matteswan State Hospital for almost 12 years and 4 months. In 1945, Victor J. Whitree was arrested at the age of 46 in the City of New York on the charge of stabbing a man named John O'Connor. Following a couple of court hearings, he pleaded guilty to assault third degree. The court suspended sentence and placed Whitree on probation. Whitree's probation, according to the State's "Code of Criminal Procedure," could be no longer than three years from December 6, 1946. Whitree violated his probation and was taken into custody on April 7, 1947 and two days later was ordered to Bellevue Hospital where he was formally examined by two of the hospital's psychiatrists. The two psychiatrists reported to the Court of Sessions that Whitree "was in such a state of insanity that he was incapable of understanding the charge, or of making his defense (pp. 491-492). The diagnosis for Whitree was "Paranoid Condition in a Chronic Alcoholic."

Whitree was transferred to Matteswan State Hospital on May 19, 1947 on the basis of the court order and the diagnosis of the Bellevue Hospital psychiatric examination. When serving under Whitree's form of sentence, the New York statutory law "required that a prisoner receive thorough psychiatric examination not less than once every two years." (p. 497). However, hospital records revealed that Whitree had not been afforded adequate psychiatric care as evidenced by his having been examined seven times in 6 years. Only three exams were of any depth, and they occurred in the first 4 months of the 6-year period.

On September 10, 1947, the hospital staff of psychiatrists held the only diagnostic staff meeting to which Whitree was presented during his entire 17–1/2 year stay at the hospital. His diagnosis at the time was reported to be "Psychosis with Psychopathic Personality, Paranoid Trends." The medical record revealed that Whitree had not been treated with any of the modern tranquilizing drugs or any of their less effective antecedents during his entire hospital stay and that such drugs were not prescribed to him until 1959. Moreover, Whitree was never exposed to psychotherapy or to psychological testing during his confinement.

On September 8, 1961, Whitree was discharged from Matteswan State Hospital with the diagnosis as "Psychosis with Psychopathic Personality, Paranoid Trends. Condition on Discharge: Improved." He was later administered a thorough and complete psychiatric examination on September 25, 1961, at Bellevue Hospital and diagnosed as "Schizoid Personality with Paranoid Feature." Moreover, he was declared not to be in a state of "idiocy, imbecility or insanity." Matteswan State Hospital stated that he was capable of making a defense on his behalf.

Court Decision

The Court of Claims trial was held on May 14, 1968 when Victor J. Whitree was 68 years old. Two of Whitree's four claims for causes of action were dismissed by the judge, but the remaining two were ruled in his favor. He was awarded $300,000 for damages suffered, moral and mental degradation implicit in such confinement, sustained pain and suffering caused by attacks and beatings from patients and guards at the hospital, and lost earnings over the period of stay at the hospital.

The main item of damage related to Whitree's false imprisonment for 12 years and 4 months. The defendant was found negligent in failing to conduct regular treatment and periodic examinations of the claimant and failure to treat the claimant's personal injuries which arose from the beating by fellow inmates and attendants.

In addition, the court reported that "the hospital record . . . maintained by the State for claimant was about as inadequate a record as they had ever examined." They found that the records did not conform to the community standards and that their records' inadequacies demonstrated improper and incompetent medical care.

Detroit Edison v. National Labor Relations Board
440 U.S. 301, 313 (1979)

In this case, the United States Supreme Court recognized the importance of maintaining confidentiality of psychological instruments. In essence, this was a case where an employer used aptitude tests in making certain promotional decisions. The union sought access to the tests to assess their fairness and assert grievances.

Court Decision

The court noted the tests had been validated and that future validity was tied to secrecy.

White v. N.C. State Board of Examiners
388 S.E. 2d 148 (1990)

In this case, the board found that a psychologist had committed various violations of the Ethical Principles of Psychologists. Between 1979 and 1982, the psychologist failed to adequately safeguard test materials and records. He misplaced a patient file, failed to inform clients of charges, and inadequately maintained accurate billing records. Also, he kept notes and tests that failed to coincide with client summary evaluations.

Court Decision

Following an administrative hearing, the board permanently revoked his license. The psychologist filed a petition requesting a reversal of the board's decision, but the court upheld the board's action. He then appealed, and the Court of Appeals of North Carolina found that the psychologist could be sanctioned for the violations on six matters and remanded the cases to the board to consider if the license should be revoked.

Susiovick v. New York State Education Department
571 N.Y.S. 2d 123 (1991)

A state-licensed psychologist agreed to provide a patient 10 psychotherapy sessions. Five were used and the patient canceled the remaining 5. The service provider billed the insurance for all 10 sessions. The insurance carrier notified the Department of Education that the psychologist had made claims for services not rendered.

Court Decision

The psychologist was found guilty of unprofessional conduct for failing to maintain proper records for the patient. His license was suspended for three months. On appeal, the court concluded that the psychologist was guilty of failing to maintain proper records.

Questions for Discussion

1. Can you really maintain confidentiality any better by not keeping records than by keeping them?
2. How might records work against your client?
3. What is likely to happen in a malpractice suit when you say you did not keep records at the request of your client but your client denies the allegation?
4. How might no record be to the client's advantage?

5. How might the record serve as a defense against malpractice?

6. How might the record assist a new therapist?

7. How might the record improve the skills of the therapist?

8. Why would an Ethics Committee or court want to review records?

9. Are there benefits to noting in the record any resistance to treatment?

10. Why wouldn't it be better to keep illegible records that could only be read by you, the therapist who wrote them? Wouldn't this protect confidentiality yet comply with the ethics codes?

11. What do you do if a group therapy client refuses to keep information confidential?

12. What do you do if you receive a subpoena ordering you to deliver records the following day?

13. What do you do if you receive a subpoena demanding you to send raw test data to another licensed professional in your state?

14. Do you think every state should have laws like New Mexico or Ohio to protect raw test data or copyright material? Does your state already have such a law?

Professional Vignette A

During the initial appointment session, a client asks you not to keep records. The client does not want his boss to know he is seeking treatment for substance abuse. The client is aware that he was referred to you by his company. He believes his boss would fire him if she were to know about his addiction. How might you deal with this request and yet follow the professional code of ethics? Would you handle it differently if your client made the request two or three months after treatment was initiated? What do you need to know about your client's right to have confidentiality maintained?

Professional Vignette B

You are served a subpoena demanding the MMPI-2 questions, the Rorschach cards, the TAT cards, and WAIS-R questions. You respond by writing the attorney, stating these materials are covered by copyright and cannot be photocopied. Furthermore, you need your originals to continue to work. You then give the addresses for the Psychological Corporation and Western Psychological Services and say, "If you want the materials, you can buy your own." What do you think about this psychologist's approach to a subpoena demanding raw materials? (Refer to Appendix K for a possible answer.)

Professional Vignette C

One psychotherapist does not record failure to follow through on suggestions nor does he keep any records of canceled or failed appointments because he does not want to write anything negative about his clients. What do you think about this approach?

CHAPTER 2

Limits of Confidentiality

We believe your client's records need special attention when issues such as child, adult, and spousal abuse are addressed in therapy. This chapter will also address how confidential these records are to insurance companies, EAPs (employee assistance programs), and HMOs (health maintenance organizations) and what to do with client logs, diaries, and other written material. Moreover, what happens when your client records are subpoenaed?

Are you aware of a client's limits of confidentiality? When must your client waive his rights in order for you to tell others what occurred or was said during the course of treatment? Do you need to document when you break confidentiality? Are you ever mandated to breach confidentiality? What do you do if you have reasonable cause to believe that your client is in such a mental condition as to be dangerous to herself or to the person or property of another? Are there any limits to confidentiality if your minor client reports that she is engaged in consensual sexual relations? These are some of the questions addressed in this chapter.

The Law and Confidentiality

You have a primary obligation to take reasonable precautions to respect the confidentiality rights of your clients. Unless the law requires you to reveal what your client has stated, you must remain silent.

There are two main types of state laws differing on the issue of confidentiality between you and your clients:

- **Nondisclosure Laws** prohibit you from revealing any information about your clients to a third party. Such a party might include a friend of yours or a friend/relative of a client.
- **Privilege Laws** pertain to giving information regarding clients in a court proceeding. Unless your client gives you permission, you cannot reveal what has transpired during the course of treatment.

Do you explain to your clients before treatment begins what your limits are for maintaining confidentiality? Do you know there are professional codes that address this issue? The 1992 APA *Ethical Principles of Psychologists and Code of Conduct* indicates that the standards call for psychologists to *discuss* the limits of confidentiality with clients (Section 5.01). Each state has its own laws covering exceptions to confidentiality. When in doubt about the laws of your state, you should contact an attorney. The courts in most states hold that you are to protect life. Thus, you are likely to discover that child abuse reporting, elder or dependent adult abuse reporting, and a Tarasoff-type duty to warn are required (see also Chapters 6 through 8). Moreover, you need to understand these limits so you can discuss them both orally *and* in writing with your clients.

The American Psychological Association (APA) Committee of Professional Practice and Standards, a committee of the Board of Professional Affairs, drafted *Record Keeping Guidelines,* which were adopted by the Council of Representatives in February 1983. Section 2, on Construction and Control of Records, parts of which appear below, makes specific reference to confidentiality:

2a. Psychologists maintain a system that protects the confidentiality of records. They must take reasonable steps to establish and maintain the confidentiality of information arising from their own delivery of psychological services, or the services provided by others working under their supervision.

2e. Records may be maintained in a variety of media, so long as their utility, confidentiality and durability are assured.

What does all this mean? You have a responsibility to maintain appropriate confidentiality in creating, storing, accessing, transferring, and disposing of client records. Data may be stored on computer. However, in the next chapter you will see that numerous items require that you maintain a paper file (e.g., all signed consents, mail received from a client or another professional, and any legal documents). Also, there is a need for a backup disk. (Think how it looks if you go to print out a copy of your record on a case only to find nothing there.) Yet with the addition of a backup disk there is added danger of possible breach of confidentiality. Some people have predicted that Managed Care will require therapists to send material via electronic communication. This might be advantageous to Managed Care, but there are definite problems regarding breach of confidentiality. When the U.S. government's computers can be entered by hackers, access to material in a psychotherapist's computer is in danger. Although it is impossible to determine and discuss all possible exceptions to confidentiality, it is clear there are some major areas to consider in your practice.

Mandatory Reporting

Duty to Protect (Warn) AKA Tarasoff (see Chapter 7)

The scope of the duty to warn has been specifically addressed, by statute or by case law, in about half of the 50 states (Ahia & Martin, 1993). When there is an identifiable victim (i.e., your client has verbalized to you whom she intends to harm) the mental health professional *must* notify the potential victim and the police in Arizona, California, Kentucky, Louisiana, Maryland, Montana, and Utah. In Minnesota, law enforcement is notified only when the identifiable victim cannot be reached. In Colorado, your client does not need to tell you he *intends* to kill a victim in order to warn. Your client only needs to tell you that he is *considering* killing the victim and that he has the ability to do it. With this amount of information, Colorado stipulates that you must call the potential victim. States that allow you a choice among responses to fullfill the duty to protect are Indiana, Massachusetts, Michigan, New Hampshire, and Tennessee. Only Indiana does not require that there be an identifiable victim. Also, the options vary from any of three or four choices, depending on the state (p. 82). We advise you to know the laws in your state.

Each state that requires you to break confidentiality has a civil code to protect you from liability. In fact, Section 43.92 of the California Civil Code covers situations in which you are *required* by law to warn a threatened victim and law enforcement:

a. "There shall be no monetary liability on the part of, and no cause of action shall rise against, any person who is a psychotherapist; as defined in Section 1010 of the Evidence Code; in failing to warn of and protect from a patient's threatened violent behavior except where the patient has communicated to identifiable victim or victims." In other words, you do not need to warn the victim if your client has already warned this person herself.

b. "If there is a duty to warn and protect under the limited circumstances specified above, the duty shall be discharged by the psychotherapist making reasonable efforts to communicate the threat to the victim or victims and to a law enforcement agency." In other words, you must make every effort to reach the intended victim. Perhaps you will need to do so in writing if you cannot reach them by phone.

Child Abuse

Since 1967, all states, including the District of Columbia, have had mandatory child abuse reporting laws. In Maine and Maryland, the law provides for discretion not to report. "All states provide *immunity* from civil or criminal liability for reporting; a majority of the states require that the report be made in good faith"

(Heymann, in Everstine & Everstine, 1990, p. 148). Not only should you follow the law, your actions need to be recorded in the client record. In California, any licensed psychotherapist who knows, or who reasonably suspects, that a child has been the victim of abuse shall report the instance to a child protective agency as soon as practically possible by telephone and shall prepare a written report (on a form provided by Child Protective Services) within 36 hours of receiving the information concerning the incident. Make a copy for your own records.

"Reasonable suspicion" means that it is objectively reasonable for you, based on your professional experience, to have entertained such a suspicion. It is not required that a child directly tells you his mother beat him with an iron rod but only that you suspect this to be the case. There is no mandatory duty to report unless the victim is still a child. So if a 19-year-old woman tells you her father is beating her daily, you are not required to report this to authorities. She is considered an adult and has the legal capability to leave home on her own. However, you might be legally mandated to report this abuse if your adult client is considered a "dependent adult" or if you are aware that this particular man currently has contact with other minor-aged children.

Miller and Thelen (1987) report that less than 50% of psychologists either are willing to report when mandated or to inform their clients about the limits of confidentiality. While laws vary from state to state, when the welfare of the child is in danger, reporting of the incident to the proper authorities is now mandatory (p. 707). Stromberg et al. (1988) indicate that 60% of the 1 million child abuse reports made each year are unfounded upon investigation. The point is that "the law has already made a value judgment in this area that it prefers false positives (overreporting) to false negatives (underreporting)" (p. 416).

We suggest that you become familiar with the person to whom you do the reporting. Visit Child Protective Services and become acquainted with a social worker you respect. If you have any questions about how the report will be reviewed or handled, you can call that individual for such information. If you explain the process to your client, you can preserve his trust in the counseling relationship.

Adult Abuse

Did you know that some states require you to report elder abuse? Does your state require you to report elder abuse? In most states, an elder is defined as anyone over 65 years of age who resides in the state. When reporting is mandated, the guidelines are generally similar to child abuse reporting.

Spousal Abuse

The California law (Penal Code 11160, 11161, 11161.9, 11162, 11162.5, 11162.7, 11163, and 11163.2) requires that a health facility, a clinic, or physician's office needs to make sure a report is filed whenever they observe or learn of a patient who is suffering from a wound or physical injury (including self-inflicted injuries) resulting from assaultive or abusive conduct. This report, made to a local law enforcement agency, may be submitted by either the psychologist or another employee and must contain (a) the name of the injured person, (b) the injured person's whereabouts, (c) the character and extent of the injury, and (d) the identity of the person who allegedly inflicted the wound.

Nonmandatory Reporting

Insurance, EAPs, and HMOs

We have yet to see an insurance form where once the insured signs, he is also authorizing the insurance company to have access to his records. Thus, when your client uses insurance to pay for therapy, he has authorized you to provide certain requested information. Such information might include diagnosis, types of interventions used, treatment plans, dates of therapy sessions, and whether the client has paid the required copayment. So even though a client is not giving permission to have access directly to her records, she is giving consent to the insurance company to have access to certain information contained within those records. You need to verbally explain this to your clients at the beginning of therapy.

Employee assistance programs (EAPs) are likely to mandate that your clients sign a form authorizing you to release certain data to them. At a minimum, this might pertain to statistical information. Some EAPs require more lengthy information regarding a client. Again, we strongly advise that you inform new clients of the limits of confidentiality before initiating treatment. Explain the types of information required by the insurance company, EAP, or health maintenance organization (HMO). If you do not know the exact information, call the client's insurance company to find out.

Client Logs, Diaries, or Other Written Material

We also want to discuss the importance of keeping written materials that your client may give to you such as diaries, logs, letters, greeting cards, audio/videotapes, or journals. You need to discuss what might happen if your client's records were ever subpoenaed. How would this client behave or react? Address the fact that whether you, the therapist, must release these materials is up to the judge. The 1987 California state law guaranteeing the confidentiality of therapist-client communications includes private writings of the patient.

Subpoenas

The method for obtaining copies of records in litigation is through service of a subpoena. Your clients need to know this in case they are involved or become involved in litigation (see also Chapter 11, Retention and Disposition of Records).

Summary

Professional guidelines and ethics codes, as well as numerous publications, call for the protection of confidentiality by the proper storage of records. However, there are "limits to confidentiality" that you should discuss with a new client before treatment begins.

Insurance companies, employee assistance programs, health maintenance organizations, subpoenas, and mandatory reporting laws all can reduce the effectiveness of keeping records confidential. When the client knows the "limits" in the beginning, she may decide not to use her insurance, EAP, or HMO. We advise that you not keep client writings (e.g., diaries, journals), which are part of their record and could be subpoenaed. However, any correspondence the client writes directly to you (e.g., letters, greeting cards), you will want to retain.

Relevant Court Cases

Schaffer v. Spicer
Supreme Court of South Dakota
215 N.W. 2d 135 (1974)

Betty Schaffer, the plaintiff, was divorced from Virgil Dornbusch in July 1965. For the next four years they fought for the custody of their three children (Betty having been granted custody in 1965).

Betty sued Dr. Edward R. Spicer, her psychiatrist, for breach of the psychotherapist-patient privilege. Defendant Spicer presented an affidavit describing his treatment of Betty Schaffer. This 8-page affidavit described Betty's hysteria, the events that led up to her three nervous breakdowns, and the shock therapy she received. Dr. Spicer claimed Betty had waived any claim to privileged communication when she discussed her mental condition as a witness in her 1965 divorce.

Court Decision

The Supreme Court of South Dakota ruled that Dr. Spicer was not permitted to waive or consent to the publication of the information in his affidavit. Therefore, Betty Schaffer successfully sued her service provider for violating the psychotherapist-patient privilege.

In re Donald PEBSWORTH
Appeal of Dr. Kersey ANITA (1983)
No. 82-2726, United States Court of Appeals, Seventh Circuit

Dr. Anita, a psychotherapist, was investigated for possible fraudulent conduct in obtaining reimbursement from medical insurance companies by submitting false patient care records. Blue Cross/Blue Shield of Illinois was subpoenaed to produce "any and all records concerning Dr. Kersey Anita." Also, the requested information included the names of some of Dr. Anita's patients.

Blue Cross and Dr. Anita opposed the government's request on the basis that the production of such records would violate the psychotherapist-patient privilege.

Court Decision

The district court held that "even assuming *arguendo* such a privilege existed, it was waived through the patient's explicit authorization of disclosure of such records to medical insurance carriers, and their consequent expectation that the confidential character of the records would necessarily be compromised pursuant to the reimbursement process" (p. 262). The district court's findings were upheld by the Seventh Circuit United States Court of Appeals.

Questions for Discussion

1. If you had a client who keeps a diary, would you, the psychotherapist, be doing anything wrong by advising the client to destroy that diary because someday it might be subpoenaed?

2. If a client talks about a crime he is planning, should you document this? Should you do anything else?

3. If a spouse or parent of a client gives you information about the client, is this material entered into the record? Is it confidential?

4. If a client dies, what happens to the record?

5. Overwhelmed with guilt, a client tells you about a crime he committed two years ago. Do you document this material?

Professional Vignette

A 17-year-old female client tells you she is having "flashbacks" of a man's hand rubbing her naked stomach. She thinks it must be her father's hand and that he probably sexually abused her when she was younger. Do you make a child abuse report based on this information? What do you write in this record? (Refer to Appendix K for a possible answer.)

PART II

The Clinical Record

This section contains three chapters. Chapter 3, "Contents of a Good Record," is the major material covered in this text. It should be noted that the data discussed in Chapter 3 is needed in private practice, in agencies, and in managed care environments. What may differ from one practice situation to another is the model or style used in the various environments. From a record-keeping perspective, Chapter 4 briefly discusses family, couple, and group therapies. Record keeping in supervision and training is covered in Chapter 5.

CHAPTER *3*

Contents of a Good Record

We have pointed out the importance of keeping records in psychotherapy and that a record can benefit both the therapist and the client. Do you know the criteria for a good record? When are you recording too many details or not enough? In this chapter, we describe in detail (a) what *not* to keep in your files, (b) what we believe are the *minimum* criteria required for a client's file to meet ethical and legal standards, and (c) the *maximum* criteria that would constitute a good record and therefore protect both yourself and your clients. Keep in mind that financial records are better kept separate from treatment records.

Material NOT to Include

Certain materials that you will receive from clients or write about your clients are best *not* included in their records. This is material that could prove to be embarrassing either to a client or to yourself. Material that has no real impact on the course of treatment and could be easily misinterpreted by outside sources (e.g., a client's relatives, lawyers, and other professionals) might include the following:

- **Personal Opinions:** Comments that you note in writing about your client, his relatives, his social worker, and others are most likely about the countertransference you are having with your client. An example might be that you're feeling hatred toward a client who reminds you of your sister. We suggest you place your comments in a personal journal. Keep this journal in a safe place. By journaling your responses you can remember them. We encourage you to discuss your issues with your supervisor or therapist. These types of written comments are referred to as "process notes."

- **Discussion of a Third Party:** We suggest you do not write down remarks made by your clients that could prove to be embarrassing to them, that defame the character of a third party, or that are truly heresy. If *how* the client discusses third persons (especially threats) is important to treatment, this would be important to include in your records. Such discussions might help you with the diagnosis or the direction of treatment.

- **Sensitive Information:** When couples/individuals discuss their sexual preferences or fantasies and the information is not relevant to diagnosis or treatment, we suggest you omit this disclosure from their records. Information that could be embarrassing to the client can be construed as an invasion of privacy if read by an outside source.

- **Past Criminal Behavior:** You are not required to write this into the record *unless* the client is seeking therapy to avoid conviction. If you determine that the client came to therapy to avoid prosecution, you will want to make note of how you determine her intent and the behavior in question.

Minimal Requirements

There is no definitive list of materials that must be included in a client's record. We suggest, however, that every record contain the following minimum criteria. Compare what you already use in your record keeping with our list:

- Identifying data
- Background/historical data

- Diagnosis and prognosis
- Treatment plans
- Informed consent
- Progress notes
- Termination summary (includes evaluation of all services, client related)

You should also keep materials considered legal in context—for example, a letter from a social worker, suicidal client, or relative of a patient; a consultation report from a psychiatrist; a subpoena; a client's drawings; or copies of insurance policies and forms. Whatever you decide as your method for keeping records, we suggest you follow the standards and guidelines advocated by your professional association (e.g., APA, AmPsyA, ACA, AAMFT, NASW, ASGW).

The Complete Record

In this section, we point out additional items beyond the minimal requirements for a more comprehensive file. Table 3.1 lists all 17 of our suggestions. You can easily check items that you currently address in your records. How do your records compare with our list? In Appendix B, a fictitious example of a complete written record is presented.

Identifying Data

APA's *General Guidelines for Providers of Psychological Services* (1987) discusses the need to include identifying data in your records. Doing so gives you or anyone who is permitted to read the file a clear understanding of who is being treated. It is an easy way to remind yourself about details that might be pertinent to treatment such as the medication a client is taking. Identifying data can be written on one page and might include the following information about the client:

- Name
- Phone number (work and home)

TABLE 3.1 Checklist for Contents of a Good Record

__ 1. Identifying Data	__10. Correspondence and
__ 2. Informed Consent/Treatment Plan	Phone Calls
__ 3. Diagnostic Testing and	__11. Suggestions/Directives
Assessment/Interview	__12. Failed or Canceled
__4. Background and Historical Data	Appointments
__5. Progress Notes	__13. Supervision
__6. Current Psychological/	__14. Prognosis
Psychiatric Evaluations	__15. Release of Information
__7. Current Medications	__16. Termination Notes
__8. Diagnosis	__17. Medicare Notes
__9. Consultations	

- Date of birth and age
- Social security number
- Gender
- Physical description
- Marital status
- Occupation
- School or education
- Children living with client (ages and names)
- Other persons living with client (ages, relationship to client, and names)
- Special interests or hobbies
- Mental health insurance company, policy number, and phone number

This information may be filled out in the waiting room by clients just prior to their first session. You might ask them to arrive 15 minutes early to complete required paperwork. Be sure to specify on the phone what their paperwork entails. Clients may share with you that they cannot read English or cannot write. If so, you will need to make other arrangements.

When clients do their own paperwork, misspellings, especially regarding names, often occur. Get complete names—first, middle, and last—which you will likely need later for insurance forms. Insurance companies also require social security numbers on all forms. When you ask for phone numbers, be sure to inquire what time is appropriate to call. Ask clients how they would like you to announce yourself, always keeping in mind the issue of confidentiality. Never assume that others know a client is in therapy. Thus when calling or leaving a message, do not say you are a therapist and avoid using the term "doctor" (if appropriate) so as to assure privacy.

The physical description you write about clients should be brief, concise, and accurate. If someone else should need to begin working with them, your identifying descriptions would be invaluable. These notations may also be useful for pre- and postevaluations and can be incorporated into mental status exams.

Obtaining names of children or other persons living with a client is especially useful if you conduct therapy within a systems framework. This information is useful, in any case, because it helps (a) assess the presenting problems, (b) understand what other variables are significant to the case, and (c) create a trusting environment with clients.

Informed Consent/Treatment Plan

Consent is informed when you discuss with your client *all* risks and outcome possibilities that can occur during therapy, including the fact that therapy does not always produce desired outcomes. For example, a client might leave her spouse instead of remaining in their marriage. When informed, your client can consent to treatment while fully knowledgable of any risks. If treatment does not demonstrate success, you will need to explore and explain this situation in an understandable way. Carefully explain the meaning of signing a consent form. Remember, *consent is voluntary.* We strongly suggest that you emphasize conditions under which confidentiality will be broken. For special cases involving treating a minor (age may vary according to state law), a prisoner, the senile or comatose, or any person incapable of understanding or comprehending necessary treatment, consent must be obtained from a legal guardian or parent. Clients who are capable of comprehending such forms (consent and client rights) need to be informed of all treatment information so as to make intelligent decisions.

We advise that you have a properly constructed form, preferably consisting of only one sheet. Informed consent should be obtained *prior* to treatment. This document must be dated and signed by the client, yourself, and a witness. Write the consent form in a language that the client is capable of understanding. Review and verbally discuss the form, taking the time to answer any questions. Present a copy for the client to review and bring to the next session if desired.

We believe that you, the therapist, need to receive your client's written consent regarding the issues that follow, in accordance with ethical codes of professional organizations that mandate informed consent. For example, the National Association of Social Workers *Code of Ethics* (1996, Section 1.03, Informed Consent) asks social workers to apprise clients of risks, rights, opportunities, and obligations associated with social services given to them. We also recommend that you document in writing when clients have been informed about such limits and their response if it is atypical. Part of informed consent includes the development of a treatment plan. A treatment plan identifies the problem, objectives, goals, therapeutic techniques, and time frame (see Appendix D).

Type of treatment. State the type of theoretical perspective you work from when treating clients (e.g., behavioral, systems, or humanistic). You especially want permission if the treatment modality is unorthodox or currently being researched for outcome data (e.g., provocative, reflective team, or primal scream). We advise that you discuss and research how this method is viewed with professionals in your surrounding community or be aware if treatment is recognized on a national level.

Time parameters for sessions. Inform your clients about the length of sessions (e.g., 45 or 50 minutes). Many clients expect a full 60 minutes and can become agitated when treatment is shorter than expected. In some cases, you may determine that treatment is 2 hours or 4 times a week.

Methods of payment. Come to a clear understanding with clients about your method of billing and the amount of payment per session. Include any exceptions such as the consequence of not arriving for an appointment. Will they be expected to pay? Are they expected to pay the full amount if they are late? May they telephone for a phone session during the scheduled appointment time? Moreover, we recommend you have in writing that it is the client's responsibility (if that be the case) to consult insurance providers to see if your services are indeed covered.

Limits of confidentiality. Advise clients of the limits of confidentiality in a given situation and of your legal requirement to report those at risk of being a harm to others or physical property and any abuse of a child, adult, or elder. Inform them of how such a report is made and to what authorities. However, always consult state laws for specifics.

Risk of life changes. Clients often have the belief that therapy will help them solve their problems, but they seldom envision the potential risks involved. These risks can range from no change due to treatment to disruptive changes such as divorce (i.e., when a client's partner will not get involved in marital therapy) or depression. Parents too should know that a teenager will sometimes act out during the early stages of treatment. It is imperative that clients consent to treatment even after learning that something could happen unlike what they are anticipating.

Qualifications of the therapist. Tell clients your professional qualifications in treating the problem they are presenting. It is important that they know whether you are a licensed therapist or being supervised while working under another's license. Inform them with a written disclosure statement about the type of professional license and degrees you have acquired. Clients need to be aware if someone else will review their case. It is possible that a client might know your supervisor or a peer supervisee. In such cases, the client may refuse to be videotaped and may even refuse to be reviewed by that particular individual.

Assessment and evaluation. If you intend to use testing instruments, include this information in the consent form. Explain the purpose and nature of the testing instrument in an understandable way and state how the client will be evaluated. Clients also need to be told if a video of them is to be retained as a part of their record. Clients can subpoena or review such material. However, if a video is to be erased, as is the case when its use is for supervision, it does not become a part of the file. Furthermore, if you intend to request records from a previous therapist or a clinical facility, think through what it would mean if the client refused consent. It is best for you to be aware of your client's prior conditions for proper assessment.

Consent for minors. The California Civil Code points out conditions under which parental consent (we suggest in writing) should and should not be obtained before you treat a minor. Treatment without consent constitutes a battery upon the child, and the professional may be sued for damages and/or disciplined for unprofessional conduct (Code 25. 8). Appendix J lists specifics concerning California statutory requirements as well as the exceptions to requiring parental or legal guardian consent when treating minors (Code 25. 9). Although minors can consent to their own treatment, the statute contains a preference for the involvement of parents, unless the psychotherapist believes it would be inappropriate. If you treat a minor under these limited circumstances, you must record if and when you attempted to contact the parents or the reason why you feel such contact would not be appropriate.

Diagnostic Testing and Assessment/Interview

Prior to therapeutic treatment, one must acquire needed information. This is usually obtained through a diagnostic interview, referred to as the initial session. Our research indicates the following three special areas of information that will assist you in making a diagnosis:

■ **Presenting complaints.** This encompasses what your client says are reasons for coming to treatment. Sometimes, the answers are broad;

sometimes, they are very specific. We believe it is important to write down the exact words given because treatment directions need to be based on your client's notion for coming to you. If your client is a minor or is incompetent, write down the exact words of a parent or legal guardian. If your direction of treatment differs from your client's wishes (she wants individual therapy and you determine family therapy will be more effective), the presenting complaint may help determine that you have indeed selected the appropriate direction that works toward alleviating the complaint.

■ **Mental status evaluation.** If you do not use a mental health status exam, we recommend at least recording that you did or did not evaluate your client to be oriented times three. In other words, you found the client able to say who she is, where she is, and the date.

■ **Any significant history.** It is sometimes important to ask clients during an initial session about certain past history (e.g., suicide or homicide attempts, substance use or abuse, victimization or abuse). We believe, however, that the collection of such information might be postponed to the second session, as we discuss below.

Background and Historical Data

We strongly advise that you include historical data as a rationale for treatment and diagnosis. This information helps remind you about significant details that may be beneficial at a later date. If you are opposed to history taking, we suggest at a minimum that you include a medical history, citing any medication the client is currently using. You might also state your rationale for not including a history as we suggest and cite resources that agree with your paradigm to demonstrate you have provided the "standard of care." Your notation will be important in the event you are subpoenaed or asked to inform insurance companies.

The most commonly described elements of a history are the following:

■ **Current problems.** Clients can help you identify specific symptoms or problems they are exhibiting at the present time. These may or may not be the same as the presenting complaint. Stated problems may include depression, panic attacks, or a lack of communication and lead to outcome goals for therapy.

- **Social or personal history.** You might write a client's history chronologically and provide dates for significant events, such as educational accomplishments. You might also mention any criminal record but are not required to do so. It is advisable to add to this section as therapy continues.

- **Developmental history.** We believe it is imperative to take a developmental history if you are working with adolescents or children. This will provide the rationale for your diagnosis. Were birth and development normal, delayed, or advanced? Were there any physical injuries or periods of unconsciousness, seizures, or major operations?

- **Marital history.** When seeing a couple, it is important to include a marital history. It may be more informative to take separate histories and then compare each person's perceptions regarding the relationship. You can use sequential dates from the onset to the present time while emphasizing significant events that appear to be related to the presenting problem.

- **Physical health.** This information helps you determine if the client's perceived problems might be related to a physical injury or condition. Knowing if your client has a health problem, takes medication, or has had an operation could affect treatment and is important to record for the record.

- **Psychiatric/psychological history.** It is vital to note that you are aware of your client's in-patient history. If your client gives no history and you discover the facts later on, note this also. Be sure to include dates, hospitals, and, if possible, names of doctors (i.e., psychiatrists and psychotherapists). Also include medications given by each physician or for each hospitalization. Why was the client hospitalized and did he know the diagnosis at the time of admission and hospital discharge?

- **Medication history.** The medical history includes prescribed medications (past and current) and the dosages. Even if you have a reservation regarding medication, you need to demonstrate you are aware of the client's medication history (see also Psychiatric/ Psychological History above). In one case, the therapist agreed with the client's choice to discontinue taking her medication. The therapist saw the client's problem as systemic and treated accordingly. The client improved. However, this therapist should have noted from a "standard of care" perspective the reason why a medical evaluation was not sought. We recommend that in similar instances you seek consultation from other professionals to determine the appropriate treatment. Such a practice strays from the medical model and yet can have validity from a family therapy perspective. The medical history should also include substance abuse, eating disorders, or other related disorders that assist you in determining your diagnosis.

- **Family history.** A family history is useful when assessing whether your client is predisposed to certain problems, such as suicide or suicide attempts, substance use or abuse, alcoholism, or schizophrenia. A genogram (intergenerational) assessment is a quick way to get important data regarding family history. You may discover other family members who need treatment or that your client's family has an influence on maintaining the current problem.

- **Work history.** It is important that you have an understanding of your client's stability in keeping a job. You also may become aware of additional supportive or nonsupportive persons in your client's life.

- **Sexual history.** This is especially necessary to document if the client's identifying problem is sexual in nature. If you know you are not qualified to treat a described disorder, we recommend that you refer your client to at least three specialists.

- **Danger to self and others, and abuse.** Because confidentiality is such an important legal and ethical issue, we advise that you document in writing these three issues in depth for each client. How have you assessed and dealt with danger to self (Chapter 6), danger to others (Chapter 7), and abuse of a child, elder, dependent adult, and spouse (Chapter 8)?

Progress Notes

Progress notes are the daily journaling you do regarding what has occurred in all your therapy sessions. The way in which progress notes are made varies vastly from therapist to therapist in private practice. Records need to contain (a) a descriptive summary of all contacts (when and who), (b) observable data (e.g., appearance, behavior, mood), (c) reactions of clients, (d) reactions of parents/guardians, and (e) significant events. You may organize your notes according to any clinical policies that apply. Pay particular attention to the following:

- **The date and type of therapy** (e.g., individual, group, couple, marital, or family)
- **Progress or lack of progress** in relation to the treatment plan
- **The degree of psychological impairment,** described in observable terms, which documents the continued need for the selected level of treatment; include frequency statements (see example in Appendix C)

Popular "progress note" models. Two popular styles for writing progress notes are the SOAP and the Problem Oriented Medical Record (POMR) methods. These notes are meant to be concise and focused but may become more detailed when issues have a legal or ethical consideration.

SOAP Method
S = Subjective:
- What did the client say?
- Thematic phrase that encapsulates the session, such as "frequent fights with spouse during past week"
- Quote from the client that is significant to the issues discussed

O = Objective:
- Significant behavior in the session
- What was observed?
- Information that supports/contradicts (i.e., congruent/incongruent statements)
- Assessment tools used—methods, tests, and questions—but not results
- Counselor intervention and client response

A = Assessment:
- Clinician's hypotheses—how do you as a clinician make sense of the reasons for subjective and objective data?

■ Explanation of history of family situations—for example, drug and alcohol use

P = Plan:
  ■ Homework assigned
  ■ Issues to be discussed
  ■ Interventions to be used

Problem Oriented Medical Record (POMR) Model
  ■ *Database:* What was said during the session?
  ■ *Problem list:* What was the problem being treated?
  ■ *Treatment plan:* What were the interventions being used that related to the problem?
  ■ *Follow-up and evaluation:* How did you follow up previous intervention success? How did you evaluate your client's progress? What are your recommendations based on the evaluation?

Current Psychological/ Psychiatric Evaluations

Any evaluations conducted (past or present) can be of great value in making your diagnosis and in formulating a therapy plan. Whenever you have a client who has the potential to do harm to self or others, we advise that you ask for additional evaluation or consultation (beside your own). This is especially true in high-risk cases where the client might benefit from medication. Another opinion denotes that you have given careful consideration to how to proceed. If you are cautious about prescribing medication, work closely with a psychiatrist who endorses your point of view and have her evaluate your client. A second opinion provides you the assurance that you are working toward the client's benefit. Be sure to document what you have done, what was recommended, and by whom. Request that any consultation or recommendation be put in writing and placed into your client's file.

Current Medications

As we stated earlier, writing up your client's medical history is imperative. We advise that your records not only show the medications prescribed but also who is prescribing them. Also make note of any possible side effects and that the client has been warned (most likely by the prescriber).

Diagnosis

According to the literature, the reliability and validity of psychotherapists' diagnoses are in question. Your diagnosis needs to be accurate because of its possible repercussion on job promotions, the outcome of a custody hearing, the length of hospital stay, and how your client's bill will be paid. If you have any doubt regarding your diagnosis, consult with other colleagues and note their agreement or disagreement and rationale for maintaining or changing your diagnosis.

You can be cited for an error in diagnosis as negligence. However, it may be considered as an error in judgment and not regligence if your assessment is proved to be the result of the following: (a) It was made on a condition where a reasonable doubt otherwise exists; (b) other experts disagree with the diagnostic procedures used, and there is no proof that your procedure is considered standard; or (c) no effort was made on your part to be fully informed about the client's condition (such as in requesting information from prior clinicians involved with your client).

We advise you to carefully examine your client's history and progress notes before making a diagnosis and make sure they are compatible. In some cases, you may want to inform your client in writing of their diagnosis since it can be an important factor in their progress. This is especially true if you are aware that others such as the client's boss or probation officer will have access to a diagnosis.

Consultations

We recommend that you consult with another therapist and establish consultation with experts as part of your ongoing practice. We believe that notes need to be made of all consultations so as to establish a professional "standard of care." Consultation is needed when therapy reaches a sustained impasse. Some (Pope, 1990; Schutz, 1982) believe this practice is one of the most efficient and beneficial means of establishing good treatment standards.

Carry out consultations in a manner that ensures privacy, avoiding public places. Name the therapist consulted, the date of the consultation, the rationale for the consult, and what was stated. We also advise that you inform the consultant that you intend to record his advice. What if he does not want to be quoted? Then ask another person to be your consultant.

Any time that you question what you are doing or wonder how you are benefiting your client is a good time to work with a consultant. If more therapists made it an ongoing practice to consult with colleagues, many would be spared litigation, administrative review, or an ethics complaint.

Correspondence and Phone Calls

We believe that you should make notation of all phone contacts and conversations (including social contacts) in connection with any client. Also, keep copies of all correspondence with the client or with respect to the client. Be sure to record the date, time, reasons for, and what transpired during these phone conversations. *Beware of cellular telephones* and the possibility that such transmission can be a breach of confidentiality. Moreover, if you are using typing or billing services, we urge that you make sure they are trained to keep material confidential.

Suggestions/Directives

We strongly recommend that you record when a client has failed to follow through on your directions or suggestions. Note the directions given and the response. This can become a diagnosis: "failure to comply." Such records can be used to (a) establish contributory negligence by the client should you be sued for negligence and (b) help you keep track of the kinds of directives the client has a tendency not to follow. This may assist you in determining future directives for the client and assist in your assessment and treatment.

Failed or Canceled Appointments

Failed or canceled appointments, along with failure to keep appointments on time, are objective behaviors that should be recorded in the client's file. These data serve purposes similar to the recording of a failure to follow directives.

Supervision

If you are being supervised for any reason (a licensing regulation, student requirement, agency policy, or insurance company demand) we recommend that you keep track of when you were supervised, what the supervisor requested of you, and what suggestions the supervisor made regarding each case. It is best to have the supervisor sign her name to the record after each session (see Chapter 5 for implications regarding this issue).

Prognosis

A statement regarding the prognosis is frequently requested or mandated by an insurance carrier or by an attorney if the client is involved in litigation. Writers (Kernberg, 1975; Strupp, 1982; Wolberg, 1977) have pointed to the therapist's personality as an essential element in the prognosis of a case. The client's willingness to come to therapy and participate is another factor. It is a helpful reminder to note how you believed (at the onset of treatment) that a client would progress.

Release of Information

You will need to prepare informed consent forms that permit you to release or obtain client information and files from specified individuals. There are do's and don'ts to follow when records are being transferred.

Things to do

■ Obtain your client's previous treatment records. It is imperative that you (with the written consent of your client) write for these records to shed light on the direction of therapy and illuminate diagnostic impressions. Failure to do so could result in responding to a client ineffectually. Perhaps the client was suicidal prior to coming to you and has not shared this information. If that client should succeed in committing suicide while under your care, you could be found negligent if you have not made an effort to obtain prior records.

■ Recognize the client's right to have copies of records made available to other therapists and pertinent persons.

■ Before releasing any information, make sure the release form contains the following:

— Signature of the client or any authorized person along with the date, year, month, and day and when the release expires

— Exact name of the provider and specific instructions of what to disclose

— Information is to be released and the purpose for this information

— Institution or persons to whom the information is to be released (include address)

— Notation for the record if the client refuses to sign consent for release

— Advice given the client about what information will be released and asking if the client has any concern regarding the released material

— Signature of clients who are minors and that of appointed guardians or parents

— Notation of the conditions under which any material will be sent by facsimile (fax), discussing with clients the limits of confidentiality involved in such a transmission, as failure to do so may result in a breach of confidentiality

Things to never do

■ Never falsify a record

■ Release any information you have obtained from another mental health practitioner. Only the original record keeper has the right to the record. We advise you to inform the requesting party that they must obtain records from the original source.

Termination Notes

It is important to write down the rationale for terminating a case. We suggest in this brief note that you include how the decision was made, what goals were attained that led to the termination, referrals suggested (for special treatment or a self-help group), the diagnosis, and the client's mental status at the time.

Medicare Notes

Since July 1, 1990, there has been a Medicare law for psychologists that requires consultation with the patient's primary care physician, *if the patient agrees.* The records must show that this was discussed with the patient and whether consent was obtained or not given. Notify the patient's physician in writing that psychotherapy services are being provided or notify by phone and chart the date, time, and to whom notification was given. If the patient does not wish you to notify or consult the physician, document this fact in the records. The Medicare law does not require that you have a physician's referral for your client.

Summary

In this chapter, we discussed 17 items we believe a psychotherapist should put in a good record along with the reasons for including these items. The issue in professional record keeping is quality of care. Good records are as much a benefit to the client as to the psychotherapist. Only through a review of the record can the services of a psychotherapist be evaluated, for example, and records that document treatment process and patient response assist in continued care, especially should there be a need for a client to see another therapist.

Relevant Court Cases

Diagnostic Error

Mrs. Kenneth Baker, as Legal Guardian of Kenneth Baker, v.
United States of America
United States District Court
226 F. Supp. 129 (Iowa, 1964)

Mrs. Kenneth Baker, serving as legal guardian for her 61-year-old husband, Kenneth Baker, filed suit against the United States. Mr. Baker was a psychiatric patient at Veterans Administration Hospital in Iowa City, Iowa, for five days when he attempted suicide by leaping into a concrete window well 13 feet deep on the grounds of the hospital. Mrs. Baker sought to recover damages for injuries allegedly sustained by her husband from the suicide attempt and for her loss of consortium.

The plaintiff charged that the physician who admitted her husband to the hospital failed to properly diagnose her husband's illness and mental condition. Mr. Baker was under the care of Dr. Schrock for approximately 60 days prior to Baker's admittance to Veterans Administration Hospital. A medical certificate by Dr. Schrock indicated that suicidal content was evident, and this accompanied Baker's application for admission.

Mrs. Baker testified that she conferred with James A. Kennedy, M.D., and informed him of her husband's suicidal tendency and that she found a gun her husband had hidden in one of the buildings on their farm premises about three weeks earlier. Dr. Kennedy interviewed the patient for an hour to an hour and a half, reviewed the admitting certificate, and met with the patient's wife and brother. Dr. Kennedy ordered that Baker be placed in an open ward on the 10th floor, based on the opinion of Dr. Kennedy that the patient did not present a suicidal risk. His placement in the open ward permitted him free access to go to the third floor for meals, to the recreational area, and to go outside and walk around on the hospital grounds.

On August 27, 1960, Mr. Baker went to the grounds immediately outside the hospital building and attempted suicide by leaping 13 feet into a concrete window well. He suffered scalp wounds, fractures to the clavicle and three ribs, and injuries to the lumbar vertebral bodies. Six hours after the incident the patient suffered a stroke, which resulted in paralysis of his entire right side.

Court Decision

The critical issue of this case was whether or not Dr. Kennedy, the admitting physician of patient Kenneth Baker, was negligent in failing to properly diagnose. The Court determined that Dr. Kennedy did not follow the standard of care required. Even though the court recognized that diagnosis is not an exact science, the judgment ruled in favor of the defendant.

North American Company for Life and Health Insurance v. Merton B. Berger
United States Court of Appeals, Fifth Circuit, Unit B
648 F. 2d 305 (Alabama, 1981)

Alleging fraudulent and negligent diagnosis, North American Company for Life and Health Insurance brought suit against Dr. Merton Berger. From 1968 through 1977, Dr. Berger served as a psychiatric consultant for several airlines. During this time, he diagnosed as "totally disabled" approximately 154 air traffic controllers on the basis of job-related anxiety and depressive neurosis. North American was the designated disability income insurance company for several of these air traffic controllers. Because of the large number of claims filed, North American decided to investigate Dr. Berger and determined that many of his diagnoses of total disability were incorrect. The insurance company then attempted to sue Berger to recover the fees that had been paid to the air traffic controllers. The United States District Court for the Northern District of Georgia ruled in favor of defendant Dr. Berger on the negligence count and the insurance company appealed.

Court Decision

The Court of Appeals held that the existence of genuine issues of facts precluded summary judgment in favor of psychiatrist Dr. Merton Berger.

The court concluded that Dr. Berger furnished information derived through error, innocently and gratuitously, instead of knowingly furnishing false information, and that does not constitute negligence.

Informed Consent

Frank J. Underwood, as Administrator of the Estate
of Shirley Underwood Dunn v. United States of America
United States Court of Appeals, Fifth Circuit
366 F. 2d 92 (Alabama, 1966)

The father (Frank Underwood) of a woman (Shirley Underwood Dunn) who was murdered by her former airman husband (Airman Dunn) brought action against the United States claiming negligence. The Dunns were married on October 1, 1955 and separated on July 7, 1962. At that time, the couple's three children were ages 2, 4, and 6. On the evening of July 24, 1962, Mrs. Dunn swore out a warrant before the police, charging that her husband had committed assault and battery upon her. Airman Dunn was arrested the following day, and on July 31, 1962, Mrs. Dunn acquired a decree of divorce.

On the evening of August 8, 1962, Airman Dunn was assigned to a psychiatric clinic and left with the noncommissioned officer in charge of the clinic, Sergeant Gerald Grover. The admitting physician and psychiatrist, Dr. Friedman, recommended that Sergeant Grover contact Mrs. Dunn to assist in making an evaluation of Airman Dunn's condition.

A day or so after Airman Dunn was admitted, Mrs. Dunn met with Sergeant Grover and revealed that Airman Dunn had hit her and attempted to attack her with a crowbar and that he had threatened her life. Sergeant Grover believed that Airman Dunn "had the potential of possibly inflicting harm on someone, himself, or her" and shared this thought with Dr. Friedman. Dr. Friedman advised Sergeant Grover not to make a written note of this as he would convey this information to the physician who would be picking up the case, since Dr. Friedman was leaving the area shortly. Dr. Friedman was in the process of being transferred when, on August 10, 1962, he referred patient Dunn and all accompanying medical records to psychiatrist Dr. Edwin Larson for care. However, Dr. Larson was not informed in any manner of Sergeant Grover's conversation with Mrs. Dunn, nor of the threats made on her life until after the homicide. On September 4, 1962, Airman Dunn secured a .45 caliber automatic pistol and shot and killed his former wife.

Court Decision

Although the United States District Court rendered a decision in favor of the defendant, the Court of Appeals reversed the judgment. The Court of Appeals held that psychiatrist Dr. Friedman was negligent for not communicating information he had known concerning Airman Dunn's threats to this former wife. Psychiatrist Dr. Larson was found not liable for negligence in releasing Airman Dunn to duty. It was recognized that Dr. Larson had not been informed of any threats that Airman Dunn had made, so there was no such information in his records.

Ethel K. Stowers v. Joseph Wolodzko
Supreme Court of Michigan
386 Mic. 119; 191 N.W. 2d 355, Nov. 9, 1971

Mrs. Stowers filed for damages as a result of her treatment during a 23-day commitment at Ardmore Acres. Mrs. Stowers stated that without her authorization, knowledge, or signed consent and at the insistence of her husband, who called the hospital, she was forced to enter an ambulance and be under the care of Dr. Wolodzko.

She stated that she was not allowed to call relatives or a lawyer while at Ardmore Acres. The defense stated that when she arrived at the hospital Dr. Wolodzko and Dr. Anthony Smyk signed a sworn statement that they had found Mrs. Stowers mentally ill and then filed for a certificate with a probate court for temporary hospitalization until a hearing regarding her sanity could be determined.

The defense noted that a judge did order that Mrs. Stowers be committed until such a determination could be made. The court granted Mrs. Stowers $40,000 in damages.

Treatment of a Minor

Dymek v. Nyquist
No. 83-1651 (Appellate Court of Illinois,
September 18, 1984)

This case demonstrates the court's disfavor to a therapist that does not abide by the civil codes in reference to informed consent when treating minors. A psychiatrist provided treatment to a 9-year-old boy who was brought to session by his mother. The father, who had custody of the boy, had no knowledge of treatment for a full year. The psychiatrist allegedly knew the mother was not the custodial parent and that there was no court permission for treatment.

Court Decision

The court held that the psychiatrist had no authority to subject the child to psychotherapy.

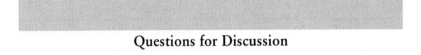

Questions for Discussion

1. What are the advantages and disadvantages in having progress notes typed into the record?

2. A psychotherapist receives a letter in the mail from a former client directing that records be photocopied and sent to a new therapist. Is this an adequate release?

3. Since there is no definitive list of materials that must be included in a client's records, wouldn't a record with just some materials be deemed adequate?

4. If a former client directs you to send the original file to a new therapist, and not retain a copy, should you do that?

5. What do you think about keeping progress notes in a computer rather than in a file?

6. What are the advantages and disadvantages in using tape recordings rather than a file to record cases?

7. Do you need a signed informed consent to tape record? What if the client refuses consent? What if the person withdraws consent and wants the tapes destroyed?

8. What are the problems with informed consent and the use of paradoxical procedures? Would it be appropriate to give only "selective disclosure?"

Professional Vignette A

A young, newly licensed psychotherapist kept records but frequently "forgot" to put identifying data on each sheet of paper in the file. When records were released to another therapist, it was noted that there were two MMPI tests and several sets of progress notes with the same dates. If you were the therapist receiving this data, what would you do?

Professional Vignette B

When a psychotherapist giving testimony was asked why there was no treatment plan in the records, she testified, "I know I did one. I must have lost it." What are the ramifications of this testimony?

Professional Vignette C

A psychotherapist indicated in testimony that he never takes a history because "it all comes out during therapy. I just wait for it to come out naturally." What do you think about this approach to history taking?

Professional Vignette D

A psychotherapist decided not to write a progress note for each session. Instead, she wrote a one paragraph summary on the last day of each month. Evaluate this approach from both legal and ethical views.

Professional Vignette E

This psychotherapist never sent for any prior psychological or psychiatric evaluations because he did not want anyone else to prejudice him regarding a case. What are the legal and ethical consequences of such an action?

Professional Vignette F

After attending a workshop where the speaker indicated that "more than one-half the people in therapy are depressed," a therapist started giving a diagnosis of depression to all his clients. He thought "making a diagnosis is not an exact science." What do you think about his approach and rationale?

Professional Vignette G

A psychotherapist has a client he feels should transfer to a new therapist but the client is very resistive to the idea. What should be recorded in the client file? Is this a good kind of a case to consult about with another psychotherapist?

Professional Vignette H

Instead of writing in notes regarding phone calls, this psychotherapist puts the phone message slips in the file. What do you think about his way of keeping records?

CHAPTER 4

Families, Couples, and Group Psychotherapy

Our thoughts regarding keeping records when one is working with a family, couple, or group grew out of discussions we had, court cases we referenced, and our consultations with clinical colleagues. Here, we touch on the more important aspects of keeping records under these circumstances that are not addressed elsewhere in the book.

Some questions to consider are as follows: If you work with couples and families or provide group therapy, how do you keep records? Do you make separate files for each client, or for the group as a whole? If you work in a hospital setting, the official policy will most often state that you are to write into the record of the identified patient (IP) what occurred in any family, couple, or group session. Most likely, the patient is being seen individually by either yourself or another assigned therapist. However, if you are in private practice you will need your own policy regarding record keeping. If you keep separate records, follow the normal policy of requiring consent before releasing the requested records. But if you keep a group file and an attorney requests your records, what should you do? We suggest you give the attorney a summary statement on the client who gave permission for release. This would include the reason for the request. However, you may still need to supply the entire file being subpoenaed.

Marital/Couple Therapy

Due to the issues of privacy and confidentiality, we suggest that you keep separate records on each spouse or partner. Even though this is an added burden, it could protect your clients' privacy. If one partner should summon your records to court, information that you may have written regarding the other partner would be kept confidential unless a client authorizes you to testify or you are ordered to testify by the court. Even if you have seen the various clients at all times together, you may have included hypotheses or generated assumptions about one partner that are inappropriate for the other to observe.

Family Therapy

We suggest that you keep a separate record for each member who has a significant role in family therapy. A member plays a significant role when he sees himself as being actively involved in treatment and does not attend on behalf of another family member. Should a family member subpoena his records, he would have access only to information pertinent to himself.

If you keep only one set of records for an entire family, who is the owner of the information? Certainly, the parents of children or adolescents have the right to access their children's records. However, if you are seeing an adult family, should all members have access to the file? We believe this would be unwise because of privacy and confidentiality issues. Ask yourself this question: Would you want members to read what you have stated about other members in the family? If the answer is "no," keep a separate file on each member.

Group Therapy

If your clients who make up a group are also seen individually in
your practice, we suggest that you keep one file on each client in
which you include information regarding any group sessions without identifying other members of the group. If clients have been
referred to take part in your group, however, we advise that you
to keep one file on the group as a whole. For daily progress notes,
write down each person's name and include the following:

- Consent forms for treatment
- Intake forms requesting background or referral information on each
  group member
- Stated goals for client
- Stated diagnosis for each client
- Verbatims regarding a client's conversation that is pertinent to
  obtaining goals
- Evaluation of a client's progress

These notes should be brief and concise. If there is "confidential"
information such as harm to self or other, write additional notes
containing what was said, how you handled the situation, and the
client's reaction. The suggestions throughout this book refer to
couples, families, and groups as well as to individuals.

Collateral Sessions

There are times during individual therapy where you may have a
few sessions with a significant other (spouse, grandparent, or some
relative). Under such circumstances, notations should be made on
a separate paper and clearly identified as collateral data. We advise
that you inform and record that you are not treating this person
who should not have to sign an informed consent nor be billed for
a session.

Summary

There are no rules or regulations for how to keep records regarding couples, families, or groups. However, you must always keep in mind the safety and privacy of your clients. Ask yourself the following questions: (a) Does this information need to be placed in the record? (b) Would I want all members of the family or couple to be reading what I am writing? (c) Can I predict what will happen to these records? If your answer is "no" to (b) and (c), we suggest you keep a separate file on each client.

Relevant Court Cases

Guity v. Kandilakis
821 S. W. 2d 595 (1991)

A man and his wife were in marriage counseling with a psychologist for over a year. There were some individual sessions, but most were conjoint sessions. During the divorce litigation, the trial judge instructed the psychologist to testify only about the joint sessions because the husband's attorney objected on the grounds of privilege. While giving testimony, the psychologist declined to answer some questions because he could not recall if the material had been dealt with in individual therapy. After the wife was awarded a divorce, the husband brought action against the psychologist, alleging disclosure of confidential information.

Court Decision

The circuit court granted the psychologist's motion for summary judgment and the husband appealed. The appeals court ruled that the psychologist was immune from suit because if he had declined to testify he would have been in contempt of court.

James W. v. Superior Court
21 Cal Rptr. 2d 169 (1993)

An 8-year-old girl complained of pain when going to the bathroom. Upon examination it was determined that she had been raped and sodomized. She indicated that a man had come through her bedroom window and hurt her. A hospital worker and detective accused her father of molesting her. A dependency petition was filed, the child was placed in foster care, and the family was referred to a private psychotherapist. At the first session, the service provider accused the father of the assault.

The family brought legal action against the psychotherapist. They alleged the therapist's accusation started a two-and-one-half year campaign to convict the father. The therapist claimed immunity under the Child Abuse and Neglect Reporting Act.

Court Decision

The appeals court of California concluded that the psychotherapist's alleged coercion of the child continued over the next two-and-one-half years. Coercion occurred long after any emergency had passed and after the authorities were actively involved, investigating and prosecuting the father. Therefore, the psychotherapist's conduct was not protected by the child abuse reporting statute.

Questions for Discussion

1. How do you keep records when you see a family or couple together?

2. What policy do you have regarding the release of family or couple records?

3. If you keep one file on a spouse, do you feel comfortable releasing records to the other spouse's psychiatrist, if you have seen them as a couple?

4. If one spouse is suing for custody of the children and you have seen them all in family therapy, do you go to court and share your records, or testify on his behalf?

5. One group member is suing another member for public slander during a group session and requests that member's file. Is there confidentiality in a group? How might your answer affect your record keeping? Consider individual records versus a group file.

Professional Vignette A

You have been seeing a couple for a year. The husband in privacy, without the wife present, told you he was HIV positive and was not going to tell his wife. A few months later they separated. The wife requested their records in regards to obtaining custody of their children. The husband did not give his permission for her to gain access. What do you do? If you had kept separate records, would the outcome be different? (Refer to Appendix K for a possible answer.)

Professional Vignette B

You have been seeing a family for a year. They originally brought in their 12-year-old daughter. Early on in treatment, she told you personal information about her friends at school, information that she did not want her parents to know. You believed that her asking to keep the information private was her way of testing your trustworthiness. Since you wanted to develop trust with the adolescent and believed this information was insignificant to the goals of treatment, the information was never revealed to the parents. The focus of treatment became the couple's marriage and not the adolescent, who improved with the refocusing of therapy. However, the couple decided to get a divorce. The husband subpoenaed the records. What do you do? Would you have written into the records what the adolescent had revealed to you about her friends? Would you have kept separate files on each member of the family?

Professional Vignette C

You have been seeing a family for 6 months. The father asks to see you privately. You have explained to the family that you do not keep secrets prior to seeing Dad separately. He tells you he has a crush on his secretary and would like help to get over his physical attraction to her. Dad loves his wife and is not sure how she will respond to his feelings for the secretary. You decide it would not be best to share this information with Mom because she is working on her self-esteem. When therapy terminates, Mother has increased her self-esteem and Dad has learned new ways of helping to support her. In addition, Dad's crush has disappeared. Two years later, their son (who attended therapy) is hospitalized for depression. The parents request their son's records. What do you do? Did you keep separate records? What policy might you have regarding the release of records?

Professional Vignette D

You have been seeing Mr. John in group therapy for 8 months. He decides to terminate. His lawyer contacts you and has Mr. John's consent for releasing his records for an impending court case. What do you do?

Professional Vignette E

A man in psychotherapy frequently brings his wife to therapy and asks the therapist to see his wife alone or insists that his wife be in therapy with him. Neither signed an informed consent for treatment. Does either the husband's or the wife's behavior constitute consent?

CHAPTER 5

Supervision and Training

A clinical arena not often discussed is how to keep records which are to be read by a third party, the supervisor/trainer. The *Ethical Principles and Code of Conduct for Psychologists* (1992) indicates that supervisors should delegate work to their supervisees that they can reasonably be expected to perform competently. Also, supervisors are charged with providing proper training and supervision, taking steps to ensure that services are performed responsibly, competently, and ethically.

The client may be aware that an additional clinician is assisting his or her therapist. Is the client also aware that this person is required to read the client's records? What problems might that present? Are supervisors required to read their supervisees' case records and to cosign supervisees' case records? Are there times when a supervisor needs to write notes in the supervisee's case records? In the following case, do you believe the supervisor provided proper supervision?

A supervisor advised a student counselor trainee to report a case involving the Mitch family to Child Protective Services (CPS). The student, without telling his supervisor, did not report the case. This student continued to see the family for the following year. At this time, CPS informed the supervisor that the Mitch family had been reported by a school counselor and wanted to know why the supervisor had not reported the case. The supervisor was stunned. What should this supervisor have done in this case? What would you have done with this case and the records?

In California, a psychological assistant must be under the direction and supervision of a licensed psychologist or board-certified psychiatrist who renders professional services at the same location at least 50% of the time during which services are rendered by the psychological assistant. Also, the supervisor must provide a minimum of one hour per week of individual face-to-face supervision to the psychological assistant. This is not true, however, for marriage, family, and child counseling trainees or interns. As of January 1, 1995, supervision must be on a ratio of 1 hour of individual or 2 hours of group supervision for every 5 hours of client contact for trainees (pre-master's degree) and 10 hours of client contact for interns (post-master's degree). Every supervisor has the responsibility (a) for the *limited* psychological functions performed by the psychological assistant, (b) to ensure that the *limited* psychological functions are consistent with the assistant's training and experience, (c) to see that the assistant complies with the provisions of the code and committee's regulations, and (d) to inform each client *in writing* prior to the rendering of services by the assistant that the assistant is unlicensed and under supervision.

Moreover, as a supervisor of a psychological assistant in California you must abide by the following:

- You must be competent to render any psychological service your assistant provides.
- Your assistant must be your employee, which is established by a W-2 form.
- There may be no family or interpersonal relationship with your assistant.
- As of July 1, 1995, you cannot supervise the same person for more than one year.

- You must notify the Board of Psychology within 30 days of termination of an assistant's employment.
- You must have a written contract with your assistant which lists unacceptable activities and practices.
- You must have regular case conferences with your assistant and review your assistant's case notes to check the client's diagnosis and look for signs of the client being suicidal, homicidal, or having sexual feelings toward the assistant.

The Board of Psychology also advises that (a) there be an informed consent statement that identifies at least the five areas required in the ethics codes, (b) any exceptions to confidentiality in California law be discussed with clients, (c) there is an initial patient history, and (d) there is a patient contract that includes an arbitration clause.

When supervising a psychotherapist in training, it is critical that the supervisor be informed about the contents of the supervisee's records. There are many considerations for this recommendation, including the fact that good record-keeping techniques are essential in these ligitious times. Other such considerations include the following points:

- Since the supervisor is legally responsible for the client's welfare, it also makes sense the supervisor is accountable for the contents of the client's records.
- Examining the supervisee's records facilitates the supervisor in accomplishing his function. The supervisor will then have a clearer perception of how the supervisee is responding to clients and progressing toward formulated goals and objectives.
- If a supervisee's case were to be brought to court, it would be imperative that notes demonstrate evidence of close and adequate supervision. In addition, if the supervisor had maintained an adequate job of reading the records, she would be prepared for court presentation.
- If any issues of confidentiality (harm to self or others) were evident in the case notes, the supervisor could be assured of how the supervisee was handling the situation.
- The supervisor might become aware of missed diagnoses or generated hypotheses from reading case notes.

- The supervisor could be assured that the supervisee has maintained appropriate record keeping procedures.

It benefits the client, the supervisee, and the supervisor to examine on a routine basis the records written by a psychotherapist in training. The client benefits because records demonstrate that the supervisor has observed the case and is aware of certain duties. The supervisor benefits when she demonstrates that a supervisee is monitoring the case closely and is working with the client. Finally, the supervisee benefits because he has proof that he is following the directives of the supervisor as outlined by the state licensing board. Supervisors are expected to do the following tasks during the supervision period:

- Sign off each week on the supervisee's records.
- Make sure that the supervisee includes in records any consultations made by the supervisor and the date when supervision occurred, or notes if supervision was missed or canceled.
- If problems arise, how they were discussed and resolved during supervision needs to be recorded.
- If the supervisee did not follow the supervisor's instruction this might also be noted in the client's notes as well as in a written summary of how the situation was resolved.

The supervisor must provide a certain amount of structure when supervising. The goals for such a structure must also be included in the client's records, such as these:

- A written contract provided by the supervisor, clinic, or supervisee's school. Such a contract usually contains agreements made between the supervisor/clinical agency and the student/school facility or supervisee. Signatures of all parties involved must be included.
- Consent forms informing the clients about the process of supervision, such as audio- or videotaping, who is observing the client (supervisor or school practicum supervisor and related students), how often the case is being reviewed, and who is basically responsible for the case. These forms must have the appropriate signatures of all parties involved.

■ Record of any meetings that occurred between the supervisor and the clients and the results of these meetings.

Summary

Supervisors often forget the importance of examining their supervisees' records on a routine basis. They need to treat these records as if they were their own. If they find that a supervisee is writing inadequate records, it is worth their time to teach the supervisee how to execute adequate record keeping.

Relevant Court Case

Cohen v. State of New York
382 N.Y.S. 2d 128 (1975)

A first-year psychiatric resident released a patient who was a documented suicide risk. The patient then committed suicide the day of release. The Court found that this unsupervised resident did not yet possess the skill or judgment to provide reasonable treatment to the decedent. In essence, any major decision the student therapist makes needs to be reviewed and altered if necessary by the supervisor.

Questions for Discussion

1. How often should the supervisor read the student counselor trainee's files of clients? What if the student counselor trainee is seeing 15 clients a week?

2. Is the supervisor basically responsible for the student counselor trainee's clients and the contents of their records?

3. If the student counselor trainee cannot write up legible records, what should the supervisor do?

4. If the student counselor trainee disagrees with the supervisor regarding an intervention, should this be noted in the records?

5. If the student counselor trainee believes that the supervisor's advice is unethical or even illegal, should this be noted in the records?

6. What should a supervisee do if her school supervisor's advice differs from her agency supervisor's advice regarding a client? Should this be noted in the records?

Professional Vignette

A student told her supervisor that she has a sexual relationship with a client. Should the supervisor record this information in the client's notes? What should the supervisor write into the client's records? Should the student write anything into these records? Should the supervisor be held responsible for the incident? Should the supervisor meet with the client and discuss the situation? Should the supervisor contact the licensing board? (Refer to Appendix K for a possible answer.)

PART III

Documentation
of Safety Issues

*T*his section consists of three chapters. Chapter 6 is concerned with danger to self, Chapter 7 with danger to others, and Chapter 8 with abuse issues.

CHAPTER 6

Danger to Self

This chapter addresses the topic of danger to self and the importance of keeping thorough documentation whenever working with suicidal clients. Whereas some therapists assume it is their professional obligation to do everything possible to keep a client alive, other therapists contend that clients are responsible for their acts. Regardless of your stand on suicide, the key questions are these: Did you know, or should you have known, of the risk? Were prudent measures used to prevent the client from committing suicide? Do you have a "standard" method for assessing lethality and for managing and documenting a suicidal client?

Assessing for Suicidal Potential

Conducting a suicidal assessment is part of administering a mental status exam, which may be divided into five major parts: Behavior, Thinking, Feeling, Data-Gathering Apparatuses, and Symptomatology. Assessing for suicidal ideation relates to focusing on the Thinking category, especially by inquiring about the client's thought content. Quite literally, you need to ask what sort of things the client thinks about and whether or not the client has any suicidal thoughts. Courts have frequently ruled that psychotherapists have a professional responsibility to assess for suicidal potential by their clients and to exercise reasonable professional care to intervene and prevent any suicidal attempts by their clients.

There are a number of risk factors to consider while evaluating a client's potential for suicide. Although there are no guarantees in predicting whether or not a client will attempt suicide, the research literature has provided us with a wealth of information about how we may assess a client's potential for suicide.

A good standard of practice is to ask all clients about suicide during the initial intake session and to *document in your records* how the client responded to your questioning. You can begin by saying that you have some standardized questions you like to ask all clients. Initially, you might ask a straightforward question like "Have you ever been so down or discouraged that you've thought about killing yourself?" If the client responds "yes," you will want to inquire more about the client's current thoughts of suicide, plan or means of suicide, previous episodes of suicidal thoughts, previous suicide gestures or attempts, and alternative means of coping (e.g., call someone for help or run away).

Many neophyte therapists have some preconceived myths about suicide. Perhaps the most serious myth is "If you ask about suicide and the client had not considered it, you are putting the idea in his head, and the client is more likely to do it." Another myth is "If I ask the client about suicide, she is going to think that I think she is really crazy or that I believe she is so hopeless that she would be better off dead." In reality, it is quite possible that by *not* asking a client about suicidal thoughts, you lose the opportunity to intervene in preventing a suicide.

Predicting Tendencies

During the course of therapy, we encourage you to be cognizant of some cues about your clients as potential for considering suicide. First, a client who reports any moderate or severe depression needs to be considered a suicidal threat. Second, a client who has recently engaged in a dangerous activity that is potentially life threatening has presented a cue (e.g., driving a motorcycle at high speed on hazardous roads). Third, a client who makes abstract or philosophical comments about death may be giving a warning signal about suicidal ideation (e.g., "He won't have to worry about me anymore because I won't be around"). Fourth, a client may convey some behavioral cues (e.g., having recently given away all of his prized possessions). You may be held liable to legal or professional sanctions if you violate the duty to predict the suicidal tendencies of your clients (see also Negligent Diagnosis below).

Suicidal Clients and the Law

There are three ways you can be legally implicated when working with suicidal clients (Ahia & Martin, 1993): assistance of suicide, negligent diagnosis, and abandonment.

Assistance of Suicide

The first issue is whether you, the therapist, did anything to assist the client's suicide. Did you intentionally ignore your professional duty to prevent it? In California, when a client threatens suicide there is no legally mandated duty to warn, as defined by the Tarasoff court ruling and the Civil Code. However, according to the appellate court ruling in *Bellah v. Greenson*, it has been established that there is a legal duty to take "reasonable steps" to prevent a threatened suicide. California Evidence Code 1024 states,

> There is no privilege . . . if the psychotherapist has *reasonable cause to believe* [italics added] that the patient is in such mental or emotional condition as to be dangerous to himself or to the person or property of another and that disclosure of communication is necessary to prevent the threatened danger.

Directing a client to commit suicide (even if done as a para-doxical intervention), encouraging the abuse of medications, or providing a client with suicidal instruments are among actions that may be considered suicidal assistance. California Penal Code 11160 states,

> Any health practitioner employed in a health facility, clinic, or physician's office who has knowledge of, or observes, in his or her professional capacity or within the scope of his or her employment, a patient whom he or she knows or *reasonably suspects* [italics added] is a person described as follows, shall immediately make a report . . . [i.e., to a local law enforcement agency]:
>
> Any person suffering from any wound or other injury in-flicted by his or her own act or inflicted by another where the injury is by means of a knife, firearm, or other deadly weapon.

Protecting against liability. Taking reasonable steps to prevent a suicide may involve a breach of confidentiality. At this time, "recent reviews have found no successful lawsuit against a psycho-therapist or counselor who breached confidentiality to protect the life of a suicidal person" (VandeCreek & Knapp, 1984, p. 51). However, there have been successful lawsuits against psychothera-pists who failed to follow standard procedures to protect the life of a client (Austin et al., 1990). When there is a high probability that the client will attempt suicide, you have the responsibility to take specific steps "to control" the client's behavior. It is especially important that your course of action be clearly stated in the client's record. Clear, specific, and objective written documentation of treatment and preventive actions taken by you are a good safeguard against liability (Austin et al., 1990). It is also important to docu-ment the client's reaction to the therapist's intervention. Contracts, including the date and signatures of both the client and therapist, in which the client agrees with the therapist not to attempt suicide should be documented in writing and kept in the client's file. You are strongly encouraged to meet and confer with other therapists for suicidal client case reviews. Whenever informing "significant others" about the client's potential for suicide, you are advised to inform the client beforehand and to document.

Whenever terminating a therapeutic relationship with a client, it is important for you to question whether the client has any intent to harm himself and to document instances where the client denied S/I (i.e., suicidal ideation). Such documentation is especially crucial before discharging a patient from hospitalization for psychiatric treatment.

Negligent Diagnosis

Whenever you fail to diagnose as suicidal a client who later commits suicide, you may be held liable for negligent diagnosis. Several demographic (age, gender, ethnicity), social, and psychological predisposing factors may be considered by the courts as one set of risk factors for evaluating a client's potential for suicide:

- Direct (e.g., "I'm going to shoot myself") or indirect (e.g., "My family would be better off if I weren't around") verbal warning
- Presence of a plan (especially one that is specific, involves a lethal method, and is a means of execution readily available to the client)
- History of previous suicide attempts (according to Pope, 1985, 80% of completed suicides have attempted suicide in the past)
- Family history of suicidal behavior
- Frequency of suicidal ideation
- Nature of suicidal ideation
- Diagnosis: depression, drug or alcohol abuse, schizophrenia, primary mood disorders, posttraumatic stress disorder
- Demographic factors: *age*—risk increases with adolescents and individuals aged 45 and older; *gender*—the suicide rate for men is about three times that for women, although women make three times as many attempts as men; *race*—in the United States, Caucasians have the highest rate; *religion*—Protestants have a higher rate than Jews or Catholics; *marital status*—separated, divorced, or widowed individuals are most susceptible > single > married; *social support*—living alone, lack of social support; and *employment status*—unemployed or retired

- Behavioral patterns: impulsivity, self-injurious, rigid thinking, isolation, getting life in order, giving away possessions, failing grades, indifferent or poor work performance, risk-taking behaviors, accidents (may be disguised suicide attempts)
- Antecedent events: recent improvement in depressive symptoms, recent major loss (job, friend, family member, personal ability) or anniversary of a loss ("anniversary reaction"), major life change (positive or negative) without adequate coping strategies, history of psychiatric hospitalization, release from hospitalization in past 6 to 12 months (suicide risk is greatest during weekend leaves or after discharge)
- Physical conditions: persistent insomnia; recent surgery or childbirth; intractable pain; presence of hopelessness, helplessness, or exhaustion; significant change in appetite (either decrease or increase), dramatic change in physical appearance

It is very important that you document in the client's record the risk categories and the warning signs you considered in assessing suicide risk for an individual client. It is also useful to distinguish between a death wish (e.g., "Sometimes I wish I would go to sleep and not wake up"), suicidal ideation, suicide gesture without intent to die, nonlethal self-destructive activity (e.g., cutting or burning skin), suicidal intent with plan, and suicide attempt *and* to document this information.

When assessing suicide risk in children, it is important to inquire about the child's belief regarding lethality of a plan or attempt. For example, one child may ingest four aspirins believing this "overdose" is lethal, whereas another child may ingest an entire bottle of medicine as an impulsive expression of anger without intending to die.

Abandonment

The mismanagement of a client diagnosed as suicidal when you, the therapist, abruptly terminate treatment, fail to respond to emergencies, or do not make arrangement for coverage for days not available may be considered abandonment, and you are more likely to be sued for malpractice. Obviously, it is important that you clearly document how you respond to client emergencies (e.g., time and content of your returned phone call, initiation for client hospitalization and your follow-up for contacting a client at the hospital) and the arrangements you've made for coverage the days you're not available. Your arrangements for coverage might include the name and telephone number of another psychotherapist who has agreed to be on call for you or the name and telephone number of the local county mental health agency. You can also mention the option for the client to call "911" in emergency situations.

Summary

It is important that you adhere to the written policies of your employing organization as well as state statutes when working with clients who have a propensity to harm themselves. You can be sued either for overreacting or for underreacting to a client's threat of suicide. You are expected to respond to a client's emergency. Therefore, when you are going to be unavailable for more than a day, you need to make arrangements to have someone else for coverage in the event of an emergency. Also, be certain to document information you gave to your clients.

Relevant Court Cases

Willie Eady, as Administratrix, etc., Appellant, v. Jacob B. ALTER et al., Respondents
Supreme Court, Appellate Division, Second Department
380 N.Y.S. 2d 737 (New York, 1976)

The Supreme Court of Kings County, New York dismissed action for plaintiff's claim to recover damages for wrongful death and conscious pain and suffering on April 3, 1975. The plaintiff later appealed, and a new trial was held on March 8, 1986. Unity Hospital was claimed to be liable for failing to properly supervise and restrain a suicial patient who terminated his life. The plaintiff's decedent was admitted to Unity Hospital on October 18, 1969, for a bronchitis ailment. Four days later, at 11:50 p.m., the decedent began behaving in a "very nervous" manner. A disturbance in his room about 1:30 a.m. on October 23 led to the transferring of the decedent's hospital roommate to another room. The intern's notation in the medical record stated "pt is getting nervous. He's shaking all body and tried to jump out from the window with the other patient in same room" (p. 739). Approximately 10 minutes after the reporting of this incident, the patient committed suicide by leaping from the window in his room.

Court Decision

The Supreme Court, Appellate Division, superseded the original order and reversed the judgment, finding Unity Hospital, the defendant, negligent in failing to provide closer supervision to the patient who committed suicide. The court held that the hospital intern's notation that the patient had attempted to jump out the window approximately 10 minutes before the suicide was "admissible to show that the patient's state of mind manifested potential to do himself harm and, when considered with testimony that patient had been inadequately restrained following reported incident, was sufficient to make out prima facie case against hospital" (p. 737).

Melanie Bellah and Robert N. Bellah, Plaintiffs and Appellants,
v. Daniel P. Greenson, M.D., Defendant and Respondent
Court of Appeal, First District, Division (California, 1977)
141 Cal. Rptr. 92

Two years after the suicidal death of their daughter, Melanie and Robert Bellah brought action against Daniel P. Greenson, a California psychiatrist who had treated their daughter prior to her death. Tammy had succumbed to a self-inflicted overdose of sleeping pills on April 12, 1973. At the time of Tammy's death, her parents were temporarily residing in New Jersey and were unaware of their daughter's suicidal tendencies.

In their action against psychiatrist Daniel Greenson, plaintiffs alleged that "[a] that defendant failed to personally take measures to prevent Tammy's suicide; [b] that he had failed to warn others (including plaintiffs) of the seriousness of Tammy's condition and her suicidal proclivity;

and [c] that he had failed to inform plaintiffs that Tammy was consorting with heroin addicts in plaintiffs' home" (p. 93).

Court Decision

The Court of Appeals held that psychiatrist Daniel Greenson was not liable for negligence relating to the suicidal death of the plaintiff's daughter. The court made reference to the 1975 landmark case of *Tarasoff v. The Regents of the University of California,* where the Supreme Court determined that psychotherapists are required to exercise reasonable care to inform the proper authorities and warn the likely victim when suspecting a client might injure another. The Tarasoff court ruling requires therapists to breach confidential communications only when there is potential risk of violent assault against another person who has been reasonably identified. There was no requirement to breach confidentiality in those situations where risk of harm is self-inflicted harm or mere property damage. Therefore, the current court case declined to further extend the holding of Tarasoff and thereby apply liability.

Dana Renee Johnson et al., Plaintiffs and Appellants, v. County of Los Angeles et al., Defendants and Respondents
143 Cal App 3d 298; 191 Cal Rptr 704 (May 1983)

As the result of a traffic violation, Mr. Johnson was arrested and detained for four days. On May 7, 1980, he committed suicide, two days after his release from jail. His wife, Dana Renee Johnson, and Mindy Lyn Johnson, his daughter, filed suit against the County of Los Angeles and sheriff's officers alleging the involved parties had violated their duties to confine, medicate, and summon medical care for Mr. Johnson during his confinement. Also, they alleged that the sheriff's officers violated their duty to warn them of Mr. Johnson's release from custody. The trial court dismissed the complaint, and the plaintiffs appealed. The Court of Appeals heard the case.

On May 2, 1980, Mr. Johnson was arrested by sheriff's officers for driving on the wrong side of the freeway. When arrested, Mr. Johnson revealed he was attempting to commit suicide and that "people" were trying to torture him or kill him and pleaded with the officers to kill him (p. 304). Mr. Johnson was charged with assault with a deadly weapon and taken to the county jail. Soon afterward, Mr. Johnson's wife, Dana, told the sheriffs that her husband was a "paranoid schizophrenic, had been repeatedly hospitalized, and required immediate medication" (Thorazine) to correct a chemical imbalance that created his aberrant conduct (p. 304). Mrs. Johnson further advised the sheriffs that her husband had suicidal tendencies requiring immediate medical attention, and should not be released (p. 304). The sheriffs replied that they understood what Mrs. Johnson had said and promised to hospitalize and medicate her husband. They also told her "not to worry or interfere" (p. 304).

Court Decision

The Court of Appeals reversed judgment of the trial court and ruled that the county had a duty to warn the released prisoner's wife and daughter. The court maintained that defendants (the county and sheriff's officer) stood in a special relationship to the decedent [Mr. Johnson] and to the plaintiffs [wife and daughter of Mr. Johnson] and thus had a duty to warn the plaintiffs before releasing the decedent (p. 298). The court found that the defendants were immune from liability for failure to confine or medicate Mr. Johnson. In the court of appeals the decision was reversed. The defendants were held liable for breaching their statutory duty of care to Mr. Johnson pursuant to a government code by failing to obtain medical care for Mr. Johnson when they knew, or had reason to know, that he was in need of immediate medical care (p. 305).

Is there a duty to warn about potential suicide? In *Bellah v. Greenson,* 141 Cal. Rptr 92 (1977), there was no duty to warn, while in *Johnson v. County of Los Angeles,* 143 C.A. 3rd 298 (1983), the court ruled that the county had a duty to warn of impending release of suicidal persons. We conclude from the two previous decisions that in California the clinician in private practice has no duty to warn about potential suicide. However, there is a legal duty to take reasonable steps to prevent a threatened suicide. In a public agency, however, the clinician *must* warn about potential suicide.

In *Currie v. U.S.,* 644 F. Supp. 1974 (1986), the U.S. District Court for the Middle District of North Carolina determined that psychotherapists have a legal duty to commit patients who present a threat to self or others. However, the legal standard supports good-faith decisions. The court noted the inherent conflict between protecting society and protecting the individual by treating in the least restrictive environment. The solution to this dilemma was to allow judgment errors in commitment decisions by creating a "psychotherapist judgment rule" where the court examines and determines the *good faith and thoroughness* of the psychotherapist in deciding not to commit. Thus, the court considered (a) relevant documents and evidence to determine if they were adequately, promptly, and independently reviewed, (b) whether the advice or opinion of another therapist was obtained, (c) whether an evaluation was made in light of proper legal standards for commitment, and (d) if there was any other evidence of good faith.

How then do you as a psychotherapist protect yourself? The answer is given by the Superior Court of New Jersey, Appellate Division in *Cowan v. Doering,* 522 A. 2d 444 (1987):

> In our view, a patient known to harbor suicidal tendencies, whose judgment has been blunted by a mental disability, should not have his conduct measured by external standards applicable to a normal adult. Where it is reasonably foreseeable that a patient by reason of his mental or emotional illness may attempt to injure himself, those in charge of his care own a duty to safeguard him from his self-damaging potential.

Questions for Discussion

1. What do you do if your client tells you he frequently rides his motorcycle at 90 miles per hour on the freeway, and what do you document in the client's record?

2. A 23-year-old female comes to see you for an initial session and shows you the cuts on her wrist that she made the day before with a razor blade while intoxicated. What do you write in her file?

3. One of your clients tells you that he has tested HIV positive and that he is considering running in front of a moving train. What do you write in his file? What will you do in this situation?

4. One of your 14-year-old clients tells you that he and his friends play "Russian Roulette" with his friend's gun. What do you write in his file? What will you do in this situation?

5. A client discloses during her initial session that she was released from the hospital 7 days ago following an attempted suicide but refuses to sign a release for you to obtain the hospital records. What do you write in the client's record?

Professional Vignette A

You have been seeing a woman as your client in treatment for 7 months. Your client's husband calls you and says his wife, who was very agitated, left the house in the car, saying that she was going to kill herself. She has tried to commit suicide before but recently appeared to be making progress in therapy. What questions do you ask the husband? What do you advise the husband, and what do you do? What, if anything, do you write in the client's chart? (Refer to Appendix K for a possible answer.)

Professional Vignette B

A very busy psychotherapist receives a request for a release of information from a former patient who had repeatedly made suicidal gestures. He intended to send significant information from his files but just never found the time to do so. Thirty days later he read in the newspaper that his former client had committed suicide. What are the legal and ethical ramifications of this case?

Professional Vignette C

A psychotherapist did not assess for suicide because the client said that "attempts to do that are in the past. A year ago, I gave all my guns away. Don't worry about me killing myself. . . . I'm here because I just got laid off at work and I need your help in how to go about finding a job." Prior to the next appointment, the client killed himself. What are the ramifications of what you recorded in the client's file?

Danger to Others

This chapter discusses the importance for you to assess for clients who may be dangerous to others and how to document such cases. The topic of violence generates a variety of concerns and emotions among psychotherapists. Some choose to deny the possibility that their clients would actually injure another person, whereas others fear for their own safety, the safety of their own families, or others in society. Since the California court 1976 ruling in the Tarasoff appeal (see Appendix A), mental health professionals have been seriously concerned about the ethical and legal ramifications of the "duty to warn and protect." Of equal concern to therapists is the potential liability in court actions in dealing with clients who are dangerous to others (Herlihy & Sheeley, 1988; Knapp & Vande-Creek, 1982; Mabe & Rollins, 1986; Mappes, Robb, & Engels, 1985; Snider, 1985; VandeCreek & Knapp, 1984).

Reducing the Risks

VandeCreek and Knapp (1993) offer some guidelines to use when working with clients who are potentially violent. The guidelines are generic risk-management techniques and may help you reduce the risks when assessing and treating clients. These techniques include "continuing education, external feedback, use of protocols, consultation, and *accurate documentation*" [italics added](p. 36). Whether you are receiving external feedback, using protocols, or seeking consultation, you want to be certain that you document in the client's record your professional course of action. Accurate documentation includes writing the assessment and treatment options in the client's record. Furthermore, the management options that have been considered for the client should be clearly stated in the client's record. Clear and specific documentation serves as a safeguard in cases where you may be questioned in court about your professional course of action (see Chapter 3).

Continuing Education

Continuing education courses may help you keep up-to-date skills in dealing with clients who are potentially dangerous to others. Certain types of client problems are more likely to be encountered by therapists who work in either inpatient or outpatient settings. For instance, most dangerous clients are seen by therapists who work in inpatient facilities, because hospitalization is one of the interventions of choice for clients with serious mental illnesses who threaten others, whereas outpatient clinics specializing in the treatment of children are more likely to deal with abusing parents. Some states have mandatory continuing education to keep psychotherapists up to date. For instance, in California, licensed psychologists have mandatory continuation prior to each two years of licensing renewal.

External Feedback

It behooves you, regardless of the setting, not to practice without receiving external feedback whenever working with potentially dangerous clients. Therapists are often not in agreement when it comes to assessing for potential danger, and no therapist has total freedom from error when assessing and treating clients.

The professional literature acknowledges the imperfection of therapists in *predicting* violence (Monahan, 1984). Nevertheless, you are expected to exercise professional care in *assessing* potential for violence. An ongoing process of systematic self- and peer monitoring and evaluation is recommended. This may include a structured consultation group, use of client satisfaction forms, interpretation of client's standardized psychological test results, or other mechanisms.

Use of Protocols

The use of a variety of protocols may also serve as helpful tools in assessing clients who are potentially dangerous to others. Protocols might include a predetermined structured interview for clients who threaten to harm others, a paper-and-pencil questionnaire that includes items about homicidal ideation, and standardized psychological tests. Of course, these completed protocols would be kept in the client's record.

Consultation

Consultation needs to be an integral part of your professional practice, regardless of the types of clients you have. Whenever you have a client who has a propensity to harm others, consultation with other professionals and documentation of the consultation in the client's record are especially important. Courts of law tend to view psychotherapists who consult with other professionals as providing clients the best standard of care.

Accurate Documentation

Finally, you should carefully document in the client's record the assessment and treatment options. Furthermore, the management options that have been considered for the client should be clearly stated in the client's record. Clear and specific documentation serves as a safeguard in cases when you may be questioned in court about your professional course of action (see Chapter 3).

Duty to Warn

Whenever you work with clients who are dangerous to others, you must refer to your respective state requirements regarding (a) the communicated threat requirement and (b) the identifiable victim requirement. Differences exist among the states concerning the circumstances giving rise to a duty to warn. According to Ahia and Martin (1993),

> As of this writing, the issue of the scope of the duty to warn has been specifically addressed, by statute or case law, in about half of the 50 states. In all but one state where the issue has been addressed, the legislature, or the courts, have determined that there is a duty to warn third parties under certain circumstances. However, there is no consensus among the states as to the particular circumstances that may trigger the duty to warn. (p. 15)

Whenever circumstances give rise to a duty to warn, you should carefully document in the client's record your professional course of action, including the exact times of your telephone calls to the police and the potential victim(s), the phone numbers you called and the names of the persons you spoke with, whether or not you were able to speak directly with the potential victim(s), and the exact information you verbalized to police and potential victim(s).

The Communicated Threat

The one state that has rejected any legal duty for psychotherapists to warn third parties is Maryland. In fact, one may be held liable for breaching confidentiality in that state even when working with a dangerous client. Seven states (California, Colorado, Kentucky, Louisiana, Minnesota, Montana, and New Hampshire) currently have statutes requiring that an actual threat be communicated directly to the therapist to trigger a duty to warn third parties (Ahia & Martin, 1993). Four states (Massachusetts, New Jersey, Oklahoma, and Rhode Island) do not require a communicated threat to trigger a therapist's duty to warn. Rather, if a patient has a history of physical violence which is known to the licensed mental health professional, and the professional has a reasonable basis to believe that there is a clear and present danger the patient will attempt to harm a reasonably identifiable victim, there is a duty-to-warn mandate. In those instances where a psychotherapist knows of a client's history of physical violence, it would be important that the information be thoroughly documented in the client's file.

The Identifiable Victim

A second duty-to-warn issue relates to the identifiable victim requirement. "All states require that the potential victim be identifiable in some way in order to trigger a duty to warn that specific person" (Ahia & Martin, 1993, p. 37). However, states differ with respect to how specifically the potential victim must be identified. While most states with duty-to-warn statutes only require that the victim be *reasonably identifiable* (California, New Hampshire, Kentucky, Montana, Massachusetts, and Oklahoma), other states require that the victim be *clearly* or *readily identifiable* (Minnesota, Louisiana, and New Jersey). A duty to warn exists in the state of Colorado only when a *specific* person has been threatened (Ahia & Martin, 1993).

It may be difficult to determine who is a reasonably identifiable victim for a dangerous client. In borderline situations, we advise you to seek professional peer consultation or supervision or to confer with an attorney and to document your course of action. The California statute limits the duty to warn to when the client is the violent party, or specifically "when the client makes a serious threat of physical violence and there is a reasonably identifiable victim or victims." The California therapist is legally mandated to make "reasonable efforts to communicate the threat to the victim or victims and to a law enforcement agency." If a client is believed to be a danger to others (with no readily identifiable victim) due to a mental disorder, a therapist has the option of getting the client hospitalized under the provisions of California Welfare and Institutions Code, Section 5150. However, when someone else other than the client is the dangerous party, the therapist does not have the legal mandate to report. The therapist should, however, encourage the client to report the threat to the police or take some other appropriate action (i.e, voluntary hospitalization, seek psychiatric consultation for medication, and so on).

California Civil Code 43.92 makes reference to a patient's threatened violent behavior and damages against psychotherapists:

(a) There shall be no monetary liability on the part of, and no cause of action shall arise against, any person who is a psychotherapist as defined in Section 1010 of the Evidence Code in failing to warn of and protect from a patient's threatened violent behavior or failing to predict and warn of and protect from a patient's violent behavior except where the patient has communicated to the psychotherapist a serious threat of physical violence against a reasonably identifiable victim or victims; and (b) If there is a duty to warn and protect under the limited circumstances specified above, the duty shall be discharged by the psychotherapist making reasonable efforts to communicate the threat to the victim or victims and to a law enforcement agency. (Added by Stats. 1985, Ch. 737)

Together with making reasonable efforts to contact the potential victim(s) and the police, document in the client's record whether or not you were able to speak with the potential victim(s).

Working With Dangerous Clients

We suggest the following guidelines for those of you who work with dangerous clients:

- Carefully document in the client's record all actions taken, including your assessment for client's dangerousness to others and all of your treatment interventions.
- Keep the client in therapy with a treatment goal of dealing with the aggression.

- Assess the client's history of violence before breaching confidentiality.
- Consider having the client get rid of any lethal weapons.
- Increase the frequency of sessions on an outpatient basis (least restrictive environment) or consider inpatient treatment (preferably voluntary by the client, otherwise involuntary).
- Encourage the client to telephone certain identified people whenever feeling an urge to harm others.
- Enlist the support of the client's family and friends.
- Have client sign a contract promising not to harm anyone else, include this contract in the client's record, and give the client a copy.
- Consider a psychiatric consultation for potential medication.
- Warn third parties only following the ineffectiveness of other actions directly involving the client.
- If warning a third party is unavoidable, disclose only information necessary to ensure the safety of the victim, including the name of the therapist, the name of the client, the name of the threatened victim, and the content of the threat. Do *not* give the police or intended victim any information about the client's diagnosis or family background.
- Use an informed consent approach by receiving the client's permission for disclosure and contacting the third party in the presence of the client.
- Consult with professional colleagues and attorneys who have expertise and experience in dealing with clients who are dangerous.

Summary

Working to assess and treat clients who pose a danger to others requires risk-management techniques. State laws differ regarding the psychotherapist's responsibilities with (a) the communicated threat requirement and (b) the identifiable victim requirement. Although there are no guarantees in *predicting* a client's violence, you are expected to exercise professional care in *assessing* potential for violence. This chapter presented several guidelines for those who work with dangerous clients, including the importance of documentation in the client's record of all actions taken.

Relevant Court Cases

Vitaly Tarasoff et al. (Plaintiffs and Appellants)
v. The Regents of the University of California et al.
(Defendants and Respondents)
Supreme Court of California in Bank,
March 2, 1975, S. F. 23042

Tatiana Tarasoff was killed on October 27, 1969, by Prosenjit Poddar. The plaintiffs in this case were the parents of Tatiana. Poddar was an outpatient at Cowell Hospital under the care of Dr. Lawrence Moore, a psychologist employed at Cowell Hospital at the University of California, Berkeley. Mr. Poddar had expressed an intent to kill an unnamed girl-friend when she was to return from a trip to Brazil. The girlfriend was easily identifiable as Tatiana. Psychiatrists Drs. Gold and Yandell had concurred with Dr. Moore's decision to commit Mr. Poddar for observa-tion, but the chief of the Department of Psychiatry, Dr. Powelson, over-ruled their decision and directed the staff not to commit Mr. Poddar. Therefore, Mr. Poddar was released. Moore had sent a letter to the chief of police asking the police department to confine Mr. Poddar. Dr. Moore also "orally notified" (p. 132) campus officers Atkinson and Teel that they should detain Mr. Poddar until they could determine whether Poddar was rational. When Mr. Poddar assured the campus officers that he would not harm Tatiana, they let him go. Dr. Powelson had asked the police to return the letter written by Dr. Moore, and he directed that copies of the letter and notes taken by Dr. Moore regarding the case be destroyed.

The plaintiffs' complaint was not that the defendants did not specifi-cally warn Tatiana, but that they did not warn the parents of the danger to their daughter. What was brought out in this case is that her parents were "those who reasonably could have been expected to notify her of her peril" (p. 139). The Superior Court of Alameda County sustained the defendants' objections. The plaintiffs then appealed the case.

Court Decision

The second trial resulted in the judgment of the first trial being reversed and the case remanded. The fact that three doctors felt that Mr. Poddar should be confined for observation suggests that there was evidence that Poddar could be suspected of carrying out his threat. The court concluded that the defendants' "failure to warn Tatiana or those who reasonably could have been expected to notify her of the peril does not fall within the absolute protection afforded by section 820.2 of the Government Code." In other words, the defendants could not be offered immunity.

Daniel Shaw v. David R. Glickman
(Personal Representative
of the Estate of Leonard J. Gallant et al.)
Court of Special Appeals of Maryland
45 Md. App. 718, 415 A, 2d 625,
June 13, 1980)

Dr. Daniel Shaw brought a suit against a "psychiatric team" because it had failed to warn him about the violent nature of Mr. Leonard Billian. Three persons involved in this case, Dr. Shaw (the lover), Mr. Billian (the husband), and Mrs. Mary Ann Billian (the wife), were all under the care of the late Dr. Leonard J. Gallant, a psychiatrist, and his psychiatric team which included a psychiatric nurse and a psychologist. Mrs. Billian had left her husband during the course of treatment, and Dr. Shaw, a dentist, and she were both nude and asleep in the same bed when confronted by Mr. Billian. The Superior Court of Baltimore City granted the defendants a summary judgment, and this was appealed by Dr. Shaw.

Court Decision

The court ruled in favor of the psychiatric team because (a) Mr. Billian had never told the team that he had any hatred or intent to harm Dr. Shaw and (b) Dr. Shaw was seen as assuming the risk of injury when he went to bed with Mrs. Billian. It was noted that the State of Maryland would have seen the team as violating the statute that "privilege against disclosure belongs to the patient, not the psychiatrist or psychologist" (p. 630). Therefore, the former judgment was affirmed.

Ruth Ann Lipari, and the Bank of Elkorn (Special Co-Administrators of the Estate of Dennis F. Lipari, Deceased, and Ruth Ann Lipari, Individually, Plaintiffs) v. Sears, Roebuck and Company (a New York Corporation), and United States of America (Defendant); Sears, Roebuck and Company (a New York Corporation, Defendant and Third-Party Plaintiff) v. United States of America (Third-Party Defendant)
United States District Court, D. Nebraska
497 F. Supp. 185, July 17, 1980, Civ. No. 77-0-458

Ruth Ann Lipari brought suit against Sears, Roebuck and Company for having sold a gun to a mental patient, Ulyssess L. Cribbs. Mr. Cribbs, a patient at Veterans Administration Hospital, went into an Omaha night club on November 26, 1977 and fired shots into the room, killing Dennis Lipari and seriously injuring Ruth Ann Lipari. Sears, Roebuck and Company then filed a third-party suit against VA Hospital for failure to detain/commit Mr. Cribbs. Mr. Cribbs had been committed to a mental institution and started day-care treatment at VA Hospital on September 23, 1977. In September, while still under the care of VA Hospital, he purchased a gun from Sears, Roebuck and Company. On October 17, 1977, Mr. Cribbs, against the advice of his doctor, removed himself from treatment.

Court Decision

According to Nebraska law, "the relationship between psychotherapist and patient gives rise to affirmative duty for the benefit of third persons, but such duty arises only when, in accordance with the standards of his profession, the therapist knows or should know the patient's dangerous propensities present an unreasonable risk of harm to others" (p. 185). The court denied the government's motion for a summary judgment and supported the plaintiffs' argument that the defendants had committed negligence by failing to commit.

Sharon Lee Doyle, Paul J. Doyle and Isabelle Doyle (Plaintiffs)
v. United States of America (Defendant)
United States District Court, C.D. California
530 F. Supp. 1278, January 28, 1982
Civ. A. No. 77-3528-RJK

The plaintiffs filed suit against the United States Army for failing to diagnose, discharging prematurely, and failing in their duty to warn potential victims about Carl Russell Carson who killed security guard James Doyle.

At the age of 19, Mr. Carson entered the army on January 31, 1975. He was stationed at Fort Polk, Louisiana, for basic training. Mr. Carson told Captain Melvin G. Engstrom that he was not pleased with army personnel because they were not teaching him quickly enough how to kill people. The captain referred him to the chaplain to whom Mr. Carson reiterated his desire to commit violent acts. The chaplain recommended that Mr. Carson see the army psychiatrist. Before seeing the psychiatrist, Mr. Carson was interviewed by three counselors who all concluded that he was not an immediate danger to others. The psychiatrist, Dr. Robert W. Johansen, concluded that Mr. Carson's statements were made in order to be released from the army. However, Dr. Johansen sent Carson to the Neuropsychiatric Ward of the Fort Polk Hospital to be observed for psychotic behavior. Dr. Johansen diagnosed Mr. Carson as having an antisocial disorder but not as being psychotic. Dr. Johansen ordered that 50 milligrams of Thorazine, an antipsychotic drug and tranquilizer, be administered to Mr. Carson four times a day. After remaining on the ward from February 13 to February 18, 1975, Mr. Carson was discharged. He went AWOL (i.e., absent without leave) after leaving the hospital.

General Haldane reviewed Carson's medical and administrative files, considered the recommendations of Captain Engstrom, and sought legal advice before he discharged Mr. Carson as being unable to adjust to the army. After his discharge, Mr. Carson went to his residence in Ventura, California, and two days later went to Ventura College where he shot Mr. Doyle, the security guard, with his rifle. It was discovered later that Mr. Carson had talked about killing his parents and had gone to the college where his father was an instructor.

Court Decision

The courts decided to follow Louisiana law even though the killing took place in California. The courts determined that they should follow the laws of the state that had the most significant relationship to the case and where negligence allegedly took place. It should be noted that

> Louisiana courts have shown great reluctance to impose liability because of a failure to protect the public from a dangerous individual. In rejecting such claims, the Louisiana courts have focused consideration upon whether defendant had any duty to protect the plaintiff and whether the breach of that duty was the proximate cause of plaintiff's injuries. (pp. 1285-1286)

Reference was made to the leading Louisiana court case concerning dangerous patients—*Cappell v. Pierson*, 15, La. App. 524, 132 So. 391 (2d Cir. 1931)—which "held that the negligent release of an apparently dangerous patient was not the proximate cause of the murder committed by the patient on the day of his release" (p. 1286).

The court discussed that Louisiana law does not recognize a duty of therapists to warn third parties of a patient's violent intentions, and even if it did, Mr. Carson never stated specifically who he intended to harm. Therefore, even though Louisiana acknowledges third-party warnings, this case would not warrant such a duty.

The plaintiff argued that had Dr. Johansen conducted his interviews differently, he would have been able to determine the extent of intent to kill. The court found that just because a patient makes threats, which is not uncommon among psychiatric patients, this does not in itself prove the patient to be dangerous. The plaintiffs felt that Dr. Johansen did not conduct a proper interview that would have given him a more correct diagnosis. The court stated that to mandate the boundaries by which a therapist should conduct an interview would violate Tarasoff's decision that therapists are entitled to broad discretion as to how they choose to examine a patient. It was noted that Carson had no history of violence and was not violent during the observation time he spent at Fort Polk Hospital. Therefore, this case did not warrant a finding of negligence.

According to the findings, there was no determination of need for hospitalization as Mr. Carson was not seen as violent during his observation at Polk Hospital or at the time of discharge.

*Steven J. Cairl et al. (Appellants) v. State of Minnesota et al. (Respondents); Mary Ann Connolly, etc. (Appellant) v. State of Minnesota et al. (Defendants and third party plaintiff, respondent), Bruce Hedge (Defendant and third party plaintiff, respondent); Ramsey County Welfare Department, (Defendant and third party plaintiff, respondent)v. Steven J. Cairl et al. (Third party defendants, Appellants)*Supreme Court of Minnesota
323 N.W. 2d 20, No. 81-437
(August 13, 1982)

The plaintiff in this case was Steven J. Cairl, who owned a fourplex where Mary Ann Connolly resided. Mr. Cairl filed suit against the State of Minnesota, the Ramsey County Welfare Department, and Bruce Hedge, the community reentry facilitator for the Minnesota Learning Center, for failure to warn them about Ms. Connolly's son's dangerous tendencies. (Tom Connolly had been known to set fires.) The Learning Center had an open-door policy as part of their treatment. Bruce Hedge drove Tom Connolly home on December 21, 1977 to spend the Christmas holidays. Bruce Hedge was specifically named because he had private insurance, and the plaintiffs claimed that he therefore waived his right to be immune from liability as governmental personnel are in such cases. On December 23, 1977, Tom Connolly set fire to the living room couch. Because of this incident, Tina Connolly was killed, Tamara Connolly was severely burned, and the property of Steven Cairl was destroyed.

Court Decision

The ruling of the first trial was that the hospital staff was not held liable by the duty to warn because Tom Connolly had not specifically said that he would injure the parties and also because his mother was aware of his potential to set fires. The court also did not find Bruce Hedges as waiving his immunity because he had obtained private liability insurance intended for his work outside the hospital. The plaintiffs appealed the District Court of Ramsey County's decision. The Supreme Court of Minnesota affirmed the District Court's decision.

Davis v. Lhim
124 Mich App. 291,
March 1993

The administratrix of the estate of Mollie Barnes filed a suit of negligence against Dr. Yong-Oh Lhim, a staff psychiatrist at Northville State Mental Hospital, for failure to warn and failure in discharging his patient, John Patterson, who then shot and killed his mother, Mollie Barnes. The Wayne Circuit Court entered a judgment against the defendant and awarded the plaintiff $500,000 in damages. Dr. Lhim appealed.

John Patterson had voluntarily committed himself to Northville on six occasions between 1972 and 1975. Mr. Patterson had symptoms of insomnia, hallucinations, and depression and was diagnosed schizophrenic. Dr. Lhim released him to the custody of his mother, Mollie Barnes. His mother, at that time, was visiting her brother, Clinton Bell. Mr. Patterson stayed with his aunt, Ruby Davis, until she could not handle him so she took him to Bell's residence. Upon entering the home of Clinton Bell, John found a handgun and began shooting it. His mother tried to take the gun from him and was shot and killed.

Court Decision

The court found that Dr. Lhim's duty to discharge was not dependent on his position at the hospital, and government immunity was not given to him. A physician at the Detroit General Hospital emergency unit noted on November 12, 1973, that "Patterson paces the floor and acts strangely and keeps threatening his mother for money" (p. 306). Also, the court felt that John left the hospital on September 2 without money, which put him in a foreseeable risk situation to commit a dangerous act. The court concluded that Mrs. Barnes was a foreseeable victim. Further, the court ruled that Ruby Davis and Exola and Clinton Bell were associated with Mollie Barnes and therefore would suffer personally from her death. Also, Exola Bell was present when her sister-in-law was shot, and from such an incident one would suffer emotionally.

Warner Chrite, Personal Representative of the Estate of Catherine Chrite, deceased, Plaintiff v. United States of America, Defendant
564 F. Supp. 324, Civ No 81-73844
United States District Court, E.D. Michigan S.D.,
May 26, 1983

Veterans Administration Hospital was sued for failing to warn Catherine Chrite about one of their patients, Henry Oswald Smith, and for failing to keep this patient from being released. Mr. Smith had been released from the Michigan VA Hospital as the state law permitted a patient to remain under their supervision for a period of not more than 60 days. To have continued hospitalization, a person must have had the court's permission by filing 15 days prior to release date. On the day of his release, Mr. Smith wrote a note stating, "Was Henry O. Smith Here Yesterday. He is wanted for murder Mother in Law" (p. 346). The hospital staff wrote down the incident but did not warn the mother-in-law, Catherine Chrite, about the threat.

Court Decision

The court found that the hospital was not negligent for failure to hospitalize the patient because there was no recommendation to keep the patient beyond the 60-day limit. However, the court ruled the hospital negligent for failure to warn Mrs. Chrite about the threatening note. Also, Mr. Smith's written note demonstrated that Mrs. Chrite was a foreseeable victim. Michigan law does not have a specific law regarding the duty to warn, but the court made its decision based on the outcome of the Tarasoff case.

Genoa M. White, Appellant v. United States of America
United States Court of Appeals, District of Columbia Circuit
780 F. 2d 97, No. 84-5645
Argued November 18, 1985, Decided January 3, 1986

On February 8, 1969, Dwayne White was ordered by the court to confinement to St. Elizabeth's Hospital. At the age of 18, Mr. White had attacked police officers and killed one when they were attempting to arrest his father. The hospital had diagnosed Mr. White as an "explosive personality" (p. 99) and concluded that he had a low tolerance for stress. Over the period of 10 years, when he was receiving treatment at St. Elizabeth's, he had demonstrated incidents of violence by assaulting fellow patients and police officers. During an authorized leave, he attempted to rob a cab driver. Also, while on an unauthorized leave Mr. White married Genoa, a former patient of St. Elizabeth's. The hospital did not find out about this marriage until three months had passed and later made notes of the incident. Although the hospital had assumed that Mr. White was leaving the grounds to visit his wife, they made no attempt to tighten his security.

Dr. Lorraine Brown, a clinical psychologist, was providing weekly treatment. During the course of therapy, Mr. White revealed a fantasy in which he shot his wife. According to Dr. Brown, Mr. White clearly knew the difference between fantasy and reality. Dr. Brown indicated that Mr. White had never assaulted women and had not been violent for a year. Therefore, Dr. Brown believed she had no obligation to warn the plaintiff of possible harm. Dr. Brown did not discuss the fantasy with hospital staff because the hospital had a policy known as a "therapist-administrator split." To ensure that the therapist and patient could develop a trusting relationship, the therapist was not involved in administrative discussions regarding patient treatment.

Six months after revealing his fantasy, Mr. White left the grounds unauthorized and went to his wife's apartment. Prior to his arrival, his wife had been drinking and had shared with him a picture of herself in a bathing suit and kimono and a man in boxer shorts. When the plaintiff turned away from the patient, he took a pair of scissors and stabbed her 55 times.

Court Decision

The U.S. Court of Appeals reversed the decision but remanded the hospital for negligence and not the psychotherapist. The court ruled that Dr. Brown had followed standard care and could not be held liable. However, the hospital was negligent because it had not followed court orders confining Mr. White at all times to hospital grounds. The hospital personnel in ther own words admitted they had suspected Mr. White was leaving hospital grounds to visit his wife but had failed to tighten security.

In re Kevin F.
213 Cal. App. 3d 178;
261 Cal. Rptr. 413 (July 1989)

In 1983, Kevin told his therapist that he had stolen some money from a home of a family friend and set the house on fire to hide evidence. Furthermore, he knew people were in the home at the time he set the fire. The therapist reported this to Kevin's probation officer and later testified about Kevin's confession. The court then committed Kevin to the California Youth Authority for a maximum of nine years. Kevin appealed.

Court Decision

The California appeals court concluded that the evidence was admissible. There is no privilege under Section 1024 of the state Evidence Code if the psychotherapist has reasonable cause to believe the client is dangerous to self, others, or property of another and that disclosure is necessary to prevent the threatened danger. The Court of Appeal noted there was "substantial evidence that the psychotherapist had reason to believe that the minor, because of a fascination with fire, constituted a danger to other residents in the program" (p. 178).

Oringer v. Rotkin
556 N.Y.S. 2d 67 (1990)

The patient threatened the life of his son's schoolmate during therapy. The psychologist informed the police that the patient was dangerous. The psychologist called the family of the intended victim and warned them. The patient had been in therapy with this psychologist for five years. The patient then brought suit against his psychotherapist on the grounds that the psychologist had communicated privileged information without authorization.

Court Decision

The court dismissed the case, and the patient appealed. The Appellate Division of the New York Supreme Court ruled that the complaint was properly dismissed. It noted that the threat of imminent and serious danger was documented in the psychologist's records.

Questions for Discussion

1. A male client tells you his wife (who is not in therapy) told him she intends to kill the president of the United States? How would you document this? Do you do anything else?

2. While conducting therapy with a couple, the wife tells you her husband (who has been incarcerated for aggravated assault) told her that he intends to kill his neighbor's dog who continues to bark loudly throughout the night. He denies the reported intention. How would you handle this situation, and what would you document in the couple's file?

3. A client tells you she has repeated fantasies of killing you. How do you respond to the client, what actions might you pursue, and what do you write in the client's record?

4. What would you do if your client told you that he was going to climb up to the top of his office building and fire his gun randomly? What would you write in the client's record? Would you do anything else?

5. Your client, a 7-year-old child, tells you that his older 16-year-old brother is planning to rob a bank with his machine gun. What would you write in the client's record? Do you do anything else?

Professional Vignette

A female client whom you are seeing in couples therapy states in front of her husband that she has been having thoughts of killing him since his extramarital affair. How do you proceed with treatment? What questions do you ask her about her thoughts? How do you assess the seriousness of her thoughts? Is this reportable? To whom would you report, and what exactly would you report? How do you document this incident in the client's record? (Refer to Appendix K for a possible answer.)

CHAPTER 8

Abuse

Since 1967, every state in the nation has had mandatory child abuse reporting laws for psychotherapists. Several states have also enacted mandatory reporting laws for psychotherapists who become aware that their elderly or dependent adult clients have been abused. Also, legislation in some states has mandated spousal abuse reporting laws.

This chapter focuses on the importance of record keeping whenever working with clients who have been victims of abuse. We discuss reporting laws for psychotherapists in California. If you are practicing somewhere else, it is important to have a clear understanding of the professional reporting duties in your state.

Child Abuse

Reporting Obligations

California Penal Code 11166 states that any *child care custodian* (including but not limited to teachers, instructional aides, teacher's aides, teacher's assistants, and school counselors) or *health practitioner* (including psychologists; licensed marriage, family, and child counselors; marriage, family, and child counselor interns; and registered psychological assistants)

> who has knowledge of or observes a child in his or her professional capacity or within the scope of his or her employment whom he or she knows or *reasonably suspects* [italics added] has been the victim of child abuse shall report the known or suspected instance of child abuse to a child protective agency immediately or as soon as practically possible by telephone and shall prepare and send a written report thereof within 36 hours of receiving the information concerning the incident. . . . "Reasonable suspicion" means that it is objectively reasonable for a person in a like position, drawing when appropriate on his or her training and experience, to suspect child abuse. . . . The pregnancy of a minor does not, in and of itself, constitute the basis of reasonable suspicion of child abuse.

Whenever you first hear from a client about having been the victim of child abuse, it is important that you document in the client's record the course of action taken. This includes noting the time, date, telephone number of Child Protective Services (CPS), and the fact that a call had been made to CPS. If you are unable to speak directly to someone at CPS because of a telephone busy signal, it is important to mention that a telephone attempt was made and that you will try calling again that same day or the following day. Any additional phone calls attempting to speak to someone at CPS should be documented.

Immunity From Liability

California Penal Code 11172 addresses the psychotherapist's immunity from liability whenever filing a required child abuse report. It is worth mentioning that as a result of the *Landeros v. Flood* (551 P.2d 389 [Cal. 1976]) court decision, psychotherapists who fail to file a mandated child abuse report are liable for any subsequent abuse that occurs to the child.

Distinctions exist between when a child abuse report is and is not mandated in the State of California. Two cases that apply to this distinction are (a) when a minor is engaging in consensual sexual relations and (b) when an adult client tells you of abuse that she or he experienced as a minor.

The age of 14 in California is when minors are able to engage in consensual sexual relations without the psychotherapist filing a mandated child abuse report. However, the situation is complex and left to the interpretation of the therapist. The consensual sex assumes that there is no coercion involved. If the minor is under age 14, a report is required, unless the minor's partner is also under age 14. If one of the minors is below age 14 and the partner is 14 or older, then there is a mandate to file a report. Difficulty may exist in determining what constitutes coercion. For instance, if a 16-year-old girl says that she is having a consensual sexual relationship with her 35-year-old gymnastics coach, it might be difficult to assume that the relationship is voluntary.

In California, when an adult client tells you that she experienced abuse as a minor, a report of the abuse reported by the client is not mandated. However, you are expected to exercise professionalism by enlisting the client's cooperation in determining the possibility that her abuser may currently be victimizing other minors. If your investigation gives you a *reasonable suspicion* of current abuse, you are mandated to file a child abuse report. You should also inform the client of her option to file a lawsuit or criminal charges against the abuser.

Child abuse reports are filed in the county of the state in which the abuse occurred. For instance, if you are seeing an adolescent in an inpatient facility that is different from the state in which the adolescent reports that he was victimized by abuse, your mandated report is filed with the county child protective agency in which the abuse occurred. The national hotline for child abuse reporting is 1-800-4-A-CHILD. Documentation of child abuse reporting includes writing in the client's record about your telephone report given to CPS (or the appropriate agency in your state) and keeping a copy of the completed written report that you mailed to CPS.

Spousal Abuse

Under California Penal Code 11160, a psychotherapist employed in a health facility, a clinic, or a physician's office may be designated to submit a written report whenever observing or learning of a patient who is suffering from a wound or physical injury (including self-inflicted injuries) resulting from assaultive or abusive conduct.

Injury Report

This report, made to a local law enforcement agency, must include the following:

- Name of the injured person
- Injured person's whereabouts,
- Character and extent of the injury
- Identity of the person who allegedly inflicted the wound

We recommend that you keep a copy of the filed report in the client's record and document in the client's record the date and time that you filed the report.

Definitions of Abuse

Important definitions that apply in California to the circumstances of abuse are these:

- **Abandonment:** "The desertion or willful forsaking of an elder or a dependent adult by anyone having care or custody of that person under circumstances in which a reasonable person would continue to provide care and custody." (Welfare and Institutions Code 15610.05)
- **Child abuse:** "A physical injury inflicted by other than accidental means on a child by another person . . . the sexual abuse of a child

. . . willful cruelty or unjustifiable punishment of a child . . . unlawful corporal punishment or injury . . . or neglect of a child or abuse in out-of-home care. Child abuse does not mean a mutual affray between minors." (Penal Code 11165.6)

- **Neglect:** Failure of any person having the care or custody of a child, elder, or dependent adult to exercise that degree of care that a reasonable person in a like position would exercise. This includes failure to assist in personal hygiene, to prevent malnutrition, to provide medical care, and so forth.

- **Physical abuse:** Physical abuse includes assault, battery, assault with a deadly weapon, unreasonable physical constraint, prolonged or continual deprivation of food or water, sexual assault, and use of physical or chemical restraint, medication or isolation without authorization or for a purpose in which it was not ordered.

- **Sexual abuse:** Sexual abuse includes sexual assault (e.g., rape and rape in concert, incest, lewd and lascivious acts upon a child under the age of 14, child molestation) and sexual exploitation (e.g., conduct involving matter depicting a minor engaging in obscene acts, including pornography, aiding or assisting, and persuading, inducing, or coercing a child to engage in prostitution or pornography).

Summary

You need to be well aware of your respective state abuse reporting laws. Although all states have mandatory child abuse reporting laws, not all states have mandatory or optional elder/dependent adult abuse and spousal abuse reporting laws. Certain circumstances mandate or require you to file a report, whereas other circumstances are considered optional or permit therapists to file a report. The importance of clear documentation in the client's record was emphasized and definitions having to do with abuse issues were given.

Relevant Court Cases

W.C.W. v. Bird
840 S.W. 2d 50 (1992)

A divorced father filed suit against a psychologist and the psychologist's employer. The psychologist diagnosed the child as having been sexually abused by his father. When the district court granted a summary judgment for the defendants, the father appealed.

Court Decision

The Court of Appeals of Texas reversed the lower court and ruled that harm to a parent arising from the misdiagnosis that the father had sexually abused his son was foreseeable, for the purpose of determining if the psychologist making that diagnosis owed a duty of care to that parent.

Sullivan v. Cheshier
846 F. Supp. 654 (1994)

The parents of a psychologist's patient brought action against the psychologist alleging that he caused estrangement of the patient from her family by implanting through hypnosis a memory of sexual abuse by her sibling.

Court Decision

The U.S. District Court for Illinois ruled against the psychologist's motion for summary judgment, indicating that a genuine issue of material fact existed as to whether the psychologist implanted the patient's memories.

Questions for Discussion

1. You have been treating a family of four, including a 13-year-old girl as the identified patient. While meeting alone with her 15-year-old brother, he reveals that he and his friends had molested his sister three years ago. What do you write in the file? Do you file a report with Child Protective Services?

2. Assume you are a psychotherapist in a state where age 14 is considered the age of legal consent for sex between minors. Your 13-year-old client tells you he is having sex with his 15-year-old girlfriend. What do you write in the record? Do you file a child abuse report?

3. You are seeing a client who reports that she punishes her child by locking him in the garage and depriving him of food and phone privileges for the day. What do you record in the file? Do you have any reporting obligations?

4. A 35-year-old client tells you that she had been abused by her parents throughout her childhood. What would you document in the client's record?

5. A 12-year-old client tells you that a 16-year-old bully frequently threatens to beat him up if he refuses to give him his school lunch money. Your client also requests that you not tell his parents because his father will call him "a sissy." Do you record this in the client's file?

Professional Vignette

You have been seeing a 16-year-old emancipated girl for 6 months in both individual and group psychotherapy. She reveals that she was sexually abused by her father for 5 years, between the ages of 5 and 10. She reports that her father is currently serving time in prison for the abuse. The client's mother calls you requesting a copy of your records while seeing her daughter. What do you do in this situation? What do you document in the records? Do you release the records? (Refer to Appendix K for a possible answer.)

PART *IV*

Special Topics Relevant to Record Keeping

*T*his section consists of four chapters. Chapter 9 discusses the treatment of minors. Access to records are discussed in Chapter 10. Retention and disposition of records are the topics of Chapter 11. Chapter 12 presents the authors' concluding comments.

CHAPTER 9

Treatment of Minors

This chapter examines the practice of psychotherapy and counseling with minor clients, which is often complex when relating to laws, ethics, and record keeping (see Appendix J). It is our intent to answer the challenging questions that follow: Can a minor child initiate psychotherapy without his or her parents' or legal guardian's consent? Are there certain ages and conditions in which a minor may initiate psychotherapy without parental or legal guardian consent? Does a minor have a legal right to refuse psychotherapy? What are the criteria for becoming an emancipated minor? Who is the holder of privilege of confidential information with an emancipated minor? Do parents have the right to request access to psychotherapy records regarding their son or daughter? Does a noncustodial parent have access to psychotherapy records regarding a minor child?

None of the questions posed above can be answered easily. First, the laws for minors vary from state to state. Second, you must carefully consider a number of factors before entering into a therapeutic relationship with a minor client. Some of these factors include "the minor's age and maturity level, the work setting and its policies, parental consent for counseling (or the lack thereof), the minor's consent or resistance to counseling, the minor's intentions, the counselor's training and practice, and state and federal statutes applicable to the specific situation" (Salo & Shumate, 1993, p. 2).

School Records

The Family Educational Rights and Privacy Act of 1974 (also known as FERPA or the Buckley Amendment) must be adhered to by all public schools and educational institutions that receive federal funding (Remley, 1993). One of the provisions of this federal statute is that parents of minors, or students who are at least age 18, have a right to review all educational records. The records must be available within 45 days after the request. Biological parents generally have the right to request parent-available school records even if the parents were never married, but stepparents do not (Remley, 1990). An exception to this right may exist if the student or parents request the counselor's case notes since no one else sees these records except the counselor (Remley, 1993).

California Statues Pertaining to Minors

Treatment Without Parental Consent

Some of the statutes pertaining to the treatment of minors without parental consent in the State of California are as follows:

> Civil Code 25.9: "When a minor is *aged 12 or over* and is determined to be *sufficiently mature* to participate intelligently in outpatient mental health treatment and (1) would present a *danger of serious physical or mental harm to him or herself or to others* without such treatment or (2) has been the *alleged victim of incest or child abuse,* the minor may give consent to the furnishing of outpatient mental health services." (italics added)

Civil Code 34.10: "A minor aged 12 or older may give consent to the furnishing of medical care and counseling related to the *diagnosis and treatment of drug or alcohol related problem.* . . . As used in this section, 'counseling' means the provision of counseling services *by a provider under the state or county* to render alcohol or drug abuse counseling services." (italics added)

Both of these statutes include the following passage:

The consent of parent, parents, or legal guardian shall not be necessary to authorize the provisions of such services. Mental health treatment or counseling as authorized by this section shall include the involvement of the minor's parent, parents, or legal guardian, unless in the opinion of the professional person who is treating the minor, such involvement would be inappropriate. Such person *shall state in the client record* whether and when [date and time] he or she *attempted to contact the parent, parents, or legal guardian* of the minor, and whether such attempt was successful or unsuccessful or the reason why, in his or her opinion, *it would be inappropriate to contact the parent, parents, or legal guardian* of the minor. (italics added)

Evidence Code 1014.5: "With respect to situations in which a minor has requested and been given mental health treatment pursuant to Section 25.9 of the Civil Code, the *professional person* rendering such mental health treatment or counseling *has* the psychotherapist-patient privilege." *(italics added)*

Access to Minor's Records

Some of the statutes pertaining to a minor patient's records in the State of California are these:

Civil Code 4600.5: "Notwithstanding any other provision of law, access to records and information pertaining to a minor child, including but not limited to medical, dental, and school records, shall not be denied to a parent because such a parent is not the child's custodial parent."

Health and Safety Code 123115: "The representative of a minor shall be entitled to inspect or obtain copies of the minor's patient records under . . . the following circumstances[:] . . . Where the health care provider determines that access to the patient records would have a detrimental effect on the provider's professional relationship with the minor patient or the minor's physical safety or psychological well-being. . . ."

Emancipated Minors

Some of the statutes in the State of California pertaining to an emancipated minor are as follows:

Civil Code 62: "Any person under the age of 18 years who comes within the following description is an emancipated minor: (a) Who has entered into a valid marriage, whether or not such marriage was terminated by dissolution; or (b) Who is on active duty with any of the Armed Forces of the United States of America; or (c) Who has received a declaration of emancipation from the superior court of the county." (A minor must be at least 14 years old before he or she can receive such a declaration.)

Civil Code 63: "An emancipated minor shall be considered as being over the age of consent for the following purposes: (a) For the purpose of consenting to medical, dental, or psychiatric care without parental consent, knowledge, or liability."

Inpatient Rights of Minors

The State of California, in conjunction with the Health and Welfare Agency and the Department of Mental Health, publishes the *Handbook of Minors' Rights,* a 21-page booklet, that is made available to minors 14 through 17 years old who receive voluntary inpatient treatment in private acute psychiatric facilities. Minors are informed on the inside of the booklet's front cover that "if you believe that you have been denied any of your rights stated in this handbook without proper procedures, you may call the patients' rights advocate in your local mental health program whose address and telephone number are on the back cover of this handbook."

The handbook explains how minors, by law, have a right to the following:

1. A clinical review
2. See a patients' rights advocate
3. Wear their own clothes
4. Keep their personal possessions
5. Keep and be allowed to spend a reasonable sum of their own money for small purchases
6. Use the phone
7. See visitors
8. Have ready access to letter-writing materials, including stamps, and to receive and send unopened mail
9. Have private storage space

The handbook also explains that the minor's parent or guardian cannot make an agreement with the facility that the minor patient does not have these rights. Although the facility staff can deny the minor's rights, they cannot deny Items 1 and 2 above. The facility must show that there is "good cause" reason to deny the minor of any right. "Good cause" reason is defined as meaning that the minor would harm him- or herself or others or seriously damage the facility if the right is not denied. Punishment, discipline, and/or staff convenience are not justifiable as "good cause."

If a minor is denied one of the rights listed above, the minor must be told the reasons why the right is being denied. The denial of the right and the reasons for the denial must be written in the minor's treatment record. The minor's rights must be returned as soon as the reasons for the denial no longer exist.

Summary

You need to be well familiarized with your respective state laws for working with minors. The best interests of the child should be your guide in deciding whether or not to grant a parent's or guardian's request to have access to the minor child's records.

Although parents (both custodial and noncustodial) and legal guardians have a legal right to access their minor child's therapy records in California, the law also permits you the right to deny parental access to records if it "would have a detrimental effect on the provider's professional relationship with the minor patient or the minor's physical safety or psychological well-being." Circumstances exist where you may see a minor without parental consent. Your course of action for working with minors must be clearly documented in the client's record. California therapists who work with minors must note in the client's record if and when they attempt to contact their parents or legal guardian or the reasons why such contact would not be appropriate. Minors are granted certain rights during inpatient treatment that cannot be taken away by their parents.

Relevant Court Case

Wisconsin v. S. H.
No. 90-0766-CR
Wisconsin Court of Appeals, Dist. IV (1990)

S. H. was charged with sexually assaulting his children and sought to compel a counseling center to provide him with copies of his children's treatment records to aid in his defense. Although he exercised a release of their records, the mother and the children's guardian asserted the psychologist-patient privilege on behalf of the children.

Court Decision

The court ruled the records were privileged and not to be released, and S. H. appealed. The appeals court upheld the trial court.

Questions for Discussion

1. What documentation would you require if a teenager identifies himself as an emancipated minor wanting to seek therapy?

2. What are the conditions in which you may do psychotherapy with a minor child without parental consent, and what would you write in the client's record under such circumstances? Who would be responsible for therapy payment fees?

3. Under what circumstances might you deny parents access to their minor child's psychotherapy records?

4. What would you do if the noncustodial parent requested a copy of your minor child client's psychotherapy records?

5. A minor child's grandparent brings the child to see you for psychotherapy. How might you obtain a valid consent?

Professional Vignette

A 16-year-old boy requests to see you for professional therapy without his parents' consent. The boy reports that he has been abusing drugs and doesn't want his parents to know. He also requests that you not tell either of his parents that you are seeing him because he doesn't want any additional stress stemming from their pending divorce and child custody battle. Will you see this boy? Why or why not? What will you document in this minor child's record? (Refer to Appendix K for a possible answer.)

CHAPTER *10*

Client Access to Records

What would you do if a client of yours comes to you and states "I want to read my records"? How would you respond? Would you be alarmed or calm about the nature of the question? The purpose of this chapter is to help you understand what rights your clients have in gaining access to their records and to offer recommendations about how you might respect these rights. Although the record is the property of the provider, records are maintained for the benefit of both the client and the psychotherapist. We also examine what might be considered an appropriate response to such a request.

Client Rights to Records

Official Guidelines for Release

Because the information contained in the record is the property of the client it must be made available to the client or a legally designated representative upon appropriate request. There are several guidelines for you to be aware of in respect to client rights to see records:

- **Psychological guidelines:** APA's (1987) *General Guidelines for Providers of Psychological Services* indicate that clients have a right to examine psychological records. It is advised that this be done in the presence of a psychologist who can explain material in a meaningful manner (see Section 2.3.7.).
- **Guidelines for social workers:** a. Social workers should provide clients with reasonable access to records concerning the clients. Social workers who are concerned that clients' access to their records could cause serious misunderstanding or harm to the client should provide assistance in interpreting the records and consultation with the client regarding the records. Social workers should limit clients' access to their records, or portions of their records, only in exceptional circumstances when there is compelling evidence that such access would cause serious harm to the client. Both clients' requests and the rationale for withholding some or all of the record should be documented in clients' files. b. When providing clients with access to their records, social workers should take steps to protect the confidentiality of other individuals identified or discussed in such records (National Association of Social Workers Code of Ethics, 1996, 1.08, Access to Records).
- **Guidelines in state laws:** These vary as to client access to records, but the trend is toward requiring that psychotherapists' records be open for inspection. Earlier, it was pointed out that in California a client has the right to a summary of her file (Quinn, 1990, p. 16). When licensed psychotherapists in California were informed about this state law, we received several phone calls questioning client access to records. Thus, it was clear to us that some psychotherapists are unfamiliar with California Health and Safety Code (CHSC) 123110 regarding patient access to health records.

CHSC 123110 provides definitions. Below are several points of the law:

- Mental health records mean patient records specifically relating to evaluation and treatment of mental disorders and includes alcohol and drug abuse records.

- The inspection and copying of clients' records is covered in CHSC 25252. In essence, any of your clients or their legal representative can make a written request to inspect or have a copy of their records. You are to permit this during business hours within 5 working days after you receive a written request. Clients may be accompanied by one other person of their choice.

- You are allowed to defray copying costs, which must not exceed the specified amount per page.

- Material copied must be transmitted within 15 days of receipt of request.

Denial of Access

When a valid request for release has been signed, you cannot refuse to send the information on the grounds that your client has not paid the bill, you do not fully understand how much the new therapist knows, or for any other reason. Remember, the information belongs to the client, not to the psychotherapist. The denial of right to inspect or copy is covered in CHSC 25253. If you determine that the access of records would be detrimental or have significant adverse risk to your client, you may decline inspection or copies. Under such circumstances, you must make a written record, to be included with the records requested, noting the date of request and reason for refusing inspection or copies along with a description of the specific adverse or detrimental consequences. However, you must permit inspection by or provide copies to a licensed physician, surgeon, or psychologist designated by request of the client. In refusing the patient the right to inspect, you must inform the patient of his right to have a licensed professional (physician, surgeon, psychologist, or clinical social worker) designated by the patient inspect or receive copies. If such a request is made, you must indicate this in the records.

Sending a Release Facsimile

There is some confusion among providers about whether a fax signature is legal. In the absence of a statute requiring a specific method, a signature may be applied to paper by any mode. However, you never should accept authorizations to release information that is sent via fax unless the release states that such *a mode of communication* is permitted. Under such circumstances, you should confirm, perhaps by phone, that the individual authorized to receive the information is at the facsimile machine when the information is sent.

Cover sheet. Before sending the release information, a cover sheet should be transmitted that includes the following:

- Sender's address, phone, and fax number
- Date and time of transmission
- Number of pages being sent
- Intended receiver's name
- Receiver's address and phone and fax numbers
- What is being sent
- A statement of confidentiality of the information
- Steps to take if the receiver is not the authorized receiver

(See Appendix H for an example of a Fax Cover Sheet)

Authorizing a Release

Any release to third parties should always be *documented in the records* you maintain. This ensures that accurate records are maintained for the protection of your clients as well as yourself. The signed document authorizing the release of records from your client should be placed with the record along with a copy of any subpoena, court order, letters of guardianship, and the like. If the release is mandated by law, a written entry in the record should be made documenting the date of release, exactly what documents or information was sent, and under what statutory provision the release was mandated.

A client may *revoke a release* or authorization at any time, and you must honor the revocation unless the material has already been sent as originally directed. Written notice of the revocation should be dated, signed by the client, and placed in the record.

Release Without Client Authorization

When can a client's records be released without the client's permission? The circumstances allowing this release are discussed below.

Implicit Authorization

Requests for release of information without the client's express authorization is permissible when information for direct client care is needed for emergency medical care. Requests via telephone or fax must first be verified for authenticity by the psychotherapist prior to releasing the information.

Release to a Medical Examiner

Circumstances surrounding the death of a client must be investigated by the Office of the Coroner. The release of information to the coroner does not require previous written authorization from the client.

Release to Other Providers

Psychotherapists often receive material from other providers and/or facilities. If these are incorporated into the record, they may be considered part of the new record or be filed as correspondence. We recommend that such data be filed as correspondence and, upon a valid request, copies of this material not be released until requests for these records are made known to the original provider or facility. This allows the originator to accurately document where and to whom these records will be released.

Release of a Minor's Records

The state legislature in California defines a minor as anyone under 18 years of age. Also, we are not talking about individuals under the age of 18 years who have legally obtained adult status in terms of consent. When a parent is still legally responsible for a minor, the parent has the authority to release the child's records. For those working with youths under the age of 18, we advise the following:

- Know your state law regarding the treatment of children.
- Verbally explain your policy and the law to both parent(s) and child at the same time.
- Have them sign a document that shows what you discussed and that they understand.
- Consider having both the parent(s) and the child sign any authorization for the release of records.

Liability for Unauthorized Release

Ethics Complaints

The unauthorized release of confidential information can subject you to an ethics complaint and/or a complaint to your licensing board and/or civil liability. For an ethics committee to review and investigate a complaint against a psychotherapist, the service provider *must be* a member of the professional organization receiving the complaint.

What might happen should you be reported to the APA for an ethical violation? The APA (1992) *Ethical Principles of Psychologists and Code of Conduct* was adopted by the California Psychological Association (CPA). If you are a psychologist who holds membership with either the APA or the CPA, that organization would have jurisdiction over you. Section 5.02 of the APA's *Ethical Principles* indicates that you have a primary obligation to respect confidentiality. Let's say your client accuses you of being unethical because you showed her records to her husband without her permission. If you are found in violation, you could receive one or more of the following directives:

- Be given a cease and desist order (i.e., stop providing services)
- Work under supervision
- Acquire additional education, training, or tutorial experience
- Undergo evaluation and/or treatment
- Be placed on probation

Along with these directives you could be involved in one of the following sanctions: (a) reprimand, (b) censure, (c) dropped from membership or expulsion, or (d) a stipulated resignation. Ethics committees have no jurisdiction over a psychotherapist's license, nor can they require a provider to refund any money.

Licensing Board Actions

Psychotherapists are required to be licensed by the state and fall within the statutory constraints imposed by that state. Grounds for initiating disciplinary action of a service provider is determined by the Board that issued the license. In California, psychiatrists are governed by the Board of Medical Examiners and psychologists by the Board of Psychology; the Board of Behavioral Sciences covers both social workers and marriage, family, and child counselors. Suspension or revocation of a license is under Business and Professions Code 4982 for clinical social workers and 4992.3 for marriage, family, and child counselors. In essence, each considers as unprofessional conduct any of the following:

- Conviction of a crime related to duties of licensee
- Securing license by fraud, deceit, or misrepresentation
- Abuse of any controlled substance or dangerous drug(s)
- Gross negligence or incompetence in the performance of duties
- Violating or attempting to violate any regulation by the Board

- Misrepresentation of type or status of license, education, or qualifications
- Impersonation of another by licensee or allowing another to use one's license
- Aiding or abetting an unlicensed person to engage in license-required conduct
- Intentionally or recklessly causing harm to any client
- Commission of any dishonest, corrupt, or fraudulent act related to qualification of functions of licensee
- Sexual misconduct with a client
- Performing or holding one's self out as able to perform services beyond the scope of one's license
- Failure to maintain confidentiality
- Disclosure of fees prior to the commencement of treatment
- Paying, accepting, or soliciting compensation for referral
- False, misleading, or deceptive advertising
- Reproduction or description in public of any psychological test or assessment device
- Any conduct in supervision that violates any regulations of Board
- Permitting registered persons under one's supervision to hold themselves out as competent beyond their level of education, training, or experience

Note: Business and Professions Code 2960 covers suspension and revocation of psychologists' licenses and covers many of the same issues discussed above.

Civil Action

The potential civil liability which psychotherapists may encounter when there has been unauthorized disclosure falls into the following three categories.

Negligence. When confidential information is released without proper authorization from the patient, through a valid court order, a valid subpoena, or released in accordance with a statute requiring or permitting the release, the duty has been breached. To maintain a civil action against a psychotherapist for the negligent release of confidential information, the client must prove that (a) a professional relationship existed, (b) the psychotherapist breached his or her duty by not maintaining confidentiality, (c) an injury was sustained, and (d) the breach was the cause for the injury. The injury or damages suffered by the patient could be loss of income or physical and/or emotional injury as a result of the disclosure.

Invasion of privacy. This means the wrongful intrusion into one's private life in such a manner as to outrage, cause mental suffering, and/or be offensive to a person of ordinary sensibilities. It is not necessary for the client to prove monetary loss or damage. Damages may be awarded for mental suffering that follows an invasion of privacy. When the intrusion is highly offensive it requires that the psychotherapist expose the private facts by communicating either to the public at large or to enough people that it is certain to reach the public. The disclosure need not be intentional but could be based on negligent acts of the psychotherapist in disclosing the information.

Intentional infliction of emotional distress. This is intentional disclosure of information by a psychotherapist who causes by the disclosure severe emotional distress to the client. The type of information must be extreme and outrageous, exceeding all bounds of decent behavior (such as disclosure that the patient has been tested positive for HIV). Damages may be awarded to the client even though there are no demonstrable injuries resulting therefrom.

Summary

In this chapter, we find that roughly half the states now have laws that permit clients to have access to their records. We have also reached the conclusion that there are some psychotherapists who do not know their state law regarding client access to records.

We urge you to become aware of your state laws. When in doubt, consult with a colleague and/or contact an attorney.

Relevant Court Cases

Cutter v. Brownbridge
228 Cal. Reporter 545 Cal. Ct. App. (1986)

Newell I. Cutter II saw Robert Brownbridge, a licensed clinical social worker, in psychotherapy between 1976 and 1982. Brownbridge told Cutter that all communications and diagnoses would be maintained in confidence.

In response to a request by Cutter's former wife, Brownbridge composed a written declaration describing his diagnosis and prognosis of Cutter along with damaging personal details. Cutter filed suit, alleging that Brownbridge violated his right to privacy. Brownbridge objected, indicating that his declaration was immune from civil liability and that he had a duty to warn because he viewed Cutter as dangerous.

Court Decision

The California Superior Court found that Brownbridge had violated his client's right to privacy and confidentiality by voluntarily publishing material about Cutter.

Jane Doe v. Joan Roe and Peter Poe
Supreme Court, New York County
400 N.Y.S. 668 N.Y. Supreme Ct. (1977)

In 1977, New York had no prior case that dealt with breach of confidentiality and had not recognized a common law right to privacy. By order of the court, pseudonyms were used for all parties. Jane Doe sued her former psychiatrist Dr. Joan Roe and Mr. Peter Poe, a psychologist.

Eight years after termination of psychotherapy with Jane Doe, Dr. Roe coauthored a book with her husband, Mr. Poe. The book reported Doe's thoughts, feelings, and emotions, her most intimate relationships, and the disintegration of her marriage. Dr. Roe contended that Jane Doe had consented during therapy to the book's publication, but the consent was never obtained in writing. Thus, it was concluded that consent had never been granted by the client.

Court Decision

The Supreme Court of New York County awarded damages to Jane Doe, indicating that the curiosity of education of the medical profession does not supersede the duty to confidentiality. The coauthors, heirs, and assignees were permanently prohibited from further distribution and sale of the book.

Watters v. Dinn
633 N.E. 2d 280
(Ind. App. 1 Dist. 1994)

Vicki Watters and David Dinn (Vicki's ex-husband and biological father of her children) were involved in a custody modification proceeding for their children. Without notice to Watters or her husband, William, a subpoena *duces tecum* (i.e., requiring witness to bring relevant documents to the court during the trial) was served to St. Francis Hospital Center for William's mental health records, which were then used in the custody case. The records indicated that William had molested a former step-daughter and was voluntarily hospitalized following his attempt at suicide.

Court Decision

The Watters brought action against the hospital and Dinn. The appeals court affirmed summary judgment for the hospital indicating that it was not liable for disclosing the records. Dinn violated state trial rules by not providing notice of the subpoena to Mrs. Watters, but the reason for his request was legitimate regarding the custody hearing, and any sanctions were available only in that hearing.

Questions for Discussion

1. What is your state law concerning client/patient access to records?
2. What if you keep progress notes on tape? Would your client have access to these tapes?
3. If you keep process notes, would your client have access to these records?
4. Is it a good idea to keep progress notes on tape?
5. Discuss having client files (except for signed releases) stored on a computer.
6. What are the pros and cons of a federal law to cover client access to mental health records?
7. What if a client takes issue with something you have written in the record and demands that you change it, but your state has no law covering this situation?
8. Is it appropriate to charge a client for the time involved in reviewing her record if your policy is that you be present to explain or answer any questions?

Professional Vignette

A psychotherapist working in a state that has no law concerning client access to records has in therapy a child whose father is in therapy demanding to see the child's records. What should the therapist do? Would it make a difference if the psychotherapist were a psychologist or a social worker? What if the parents were divorced and had joint custody but the mother brought the child in for therapy and paid for all services? Would that matter? (Refer to Appendix K for a possible answer.)

CHAPTER 11

Retention and Disposition of Records

The purpose of this chapter is to ascertain what a clinician's responsibility is regarding records when a treatment has terminated. Are there any legal rulings regarding maintenance of records? How long do you store a client's records posttermination? We also discuss what considerations the therapist might address when the time is appropriate to dispose of a client's records. We hope to demonstrate that clients benefit when a mental health practitioner considers an effective method for dealing with these issues.

Official Guidelines for Retention

Several professional associations have produced written guidelines for retention. For example,

American Psychological Association *General Guidelines for Providers of Psychological Services* (1987, sect. 2.3.6): This states that psychologists need to "follow an established policy" for retention. It is indicated (sect. 2.3.7) that records are the property of the psychologist (or facility where the psychologist works).

American Psychological Association *Specialty Guidelines for Delivery of Services* (1981, sect. 2.3.4): This notes that policy on record retention must conform to state statutes where applicable. (If there are no statutes, then records should be retained for 3 years and then a summary or the full record for 12 more years). In California, health service providers are required to preserve records for a minimum of 7 years following discharge of the client; except that the records of unemancipated minors shall be kept at least one year after the minor has reached the age of 18 years and in any case not less than 7 years (Cal. Health & Safety Code 123145).

Counseling Psychology Specialty Guidelines: These recommend that if there are no regulations, then maintain records for 14 years. A complete record or summary should be maintained for an additional 3 years.

American Counseling Association *Code of Ethics and Standards of Practice* (1995, sect. B.4.a): The *Requirement of Records* states that counselors are to maintain records "necessary for rendering professional services to their clients and as required by laws, regulations, or agency or institution procedures."

AAMFT (American Association for Marriage and Family Therapy) *Code of Ethics* (1991): This code recommends that client records be stored in ways that maintain confidentiality.

State laws. From a national point of view, there is no exact answer on how long to keep records. State laws differ and, for the most part, mainly point to the length of keeping "hospital records." Different state laws suggest the following:

- California — 7 years but not before the client is age 18
- Massachusetts — 30 years

- New York — 6 years
- Nevada — 5 years
- Pennsylvania — 15 years
- South Dakota — permanently
- Texas — 10 years

In California, all licensed mental health professionals are required to keep complete records for 7 years.

Special Requirements for Storage

Business records. Business records should be retained in accordance with the Internal Revenue Service except when state law requires a longer period of retention.

Health maintenance organizations (HMOs) and PPOs. Third-party payers may dictate retention. HMOs and PPOs usually have rigorous utilization review and quality assurance mechanisms. This is done in retrospect where client records are assessed to evaluate services. In California, where psychologists work with the Medi-Cal program, they are required to keep all client records as well as their appointment book for a period of 3 years. However, the California law of 7 years prevails.

Client welfare. We believe that another consideration one should keep in mind is the needs of the client. What are the risks of maintaining records that are out-of-date and contain potentially harmful data (but are no longer relevant to the client)? In addition, these records might be passed on to another psychotherapist should the therapist become deceased. We have discussed the many ways records can benefit a client, such as providing continuity of care. If a client should leave your care and later on return to treatment with another psychotherapist, you might be required to document certain aspects of treatment. Your records will give you that important information that can provide the continuity needed to establish optimum client care.

Tips for proper storage. Earlier, we pointed to APA Standard 2.3.7. that "psychologists establish and maintain a system that protects the confidentiality of their users' records (see Chapter 2). Confidentiality of records is not limited to psychology. The American Association for Marriage and Family Therapy (1988) indicates that client records be stored in a way so as to maintain confidentiality (p. 3). Its *Principles of Medical Ethics, with Annotations Especially Application to Psychiatry, the American Psychiatric Association (1989)* charges that psychiatric records must be protected with extreme care (p. 410). What is meant by extreme care? We believe the following precautions must be observed:

- Keep files in a sturdy file cabinet that can be locked.
- Keep your records stored out of sight of unauthorized persons.
- Your *will* should authorize certain persons to maintain your records.

Disposition

Official Guidelines for Disposition

Once you have decided it is time to discard your records, how do you dispose of them properly? There are guidelines provided by various professional associations that suggest the following:

AAMFT *Code of Ethics* (1991, sect. 2.3): "Marriage and family therapists store or dispose of client records in ways that maintain confidentiality."

American Counseling Association *Code of Ethics and Standards of Practice* (1995, sect. B.4.b): This also emphasizes the importance of maintaining "confidentiality of any counseling records they [counselors] create, maintain, transfer, or destroy whether the records are written, taped, computerized, or stored in any other medium."

How to Dispose

When records are considered obsolete, you will need to shred, burn, recycle, or use some other means to destroy your records. You may contract with an outside company, but remember, if you have someone else destroy your client records, you are still responsible for maintaining confidentiality. If you have large volumes of records to be destroyed, consider investing in your own shredding machine.

Summary

We believe that the welfare of the client involves record retention. It is clear from both standards and ethics codes that records need to be maintained in a way that ensures confidentiality. How long records need to be retained is a matter of state law and the reader is advised to find out that information and recognize such regulations vary from state to state. When in doubt, consult with an attorney.

Guidelines for the disposition of records are provided by professional associations as well as through professional commentary. After records have been held for the required period, they need to be destroyed in a method that preserves confidentiality. In the event of the death or retirement of the psychotherapist, provisions should be made so that records are transferred to a designated therapist or one chosen by the client.

Relevant Court Case

Estate of Finkle
385 N.Y.S. 2d 343 (1977)

Prior to psychiatrist Finkle's death, he instructed his executor to sell his practice and gave the keys to his office to Dr. Jones, a fellow psychiatrist. Following Finkle's death, Dr. Jones treated those patients needing prompt medical attention. After getting the keys from Dr. Jones, the executor found all of Finkle's medical records missing. So that the estate could collect debts, the executor demanded that Dr. Jones return the records. Legal action ensued when Dr. Jones refused.

Court Decision

It was ruled that Dr. Jones was not entitled to possession of the records. Any loss as the result of Dr. Jones's retention of the records was a matter of fact to be determined at trial.

Questions for Discussion

1. What are the advantages for keeping records for 30 years or more? The disadvantages?

2. How do you determine when something is obsolete?

3. If you are going to destroy records but keep a summary, how extensive should this summary be? Is one paragraph enough?

4. If records are the property of the psychotherapist, why can't the therapist determine how long to keep records?

5. When the psychotherapist dies, can it be stipulated in her will that all records are to be destroyed?

6. Is it a good idea for a psychotherapist to discuss in his will what to do with his records?

7. Do you think it is a good idea for a psychotherapist to contract to have records destroyed?

8. If a psychotherapist destroys obsolete parts of a record, would that not be considered destroying evidence if there was later legal action?

9. What do you think of the idea of stamping OBSOLETE on any outdated parts of a records until the required time has elapsed and the whole record is destroyed?

Professional Vignette A

A psychotherapist decides to destroy all records three or more years old. She does not know her state law. If challenged, she will say the records were "obsolete." What do you think about this approach? Is this within your state law? Is this within the standard of care for your profession?

Professional Vignette B

A psychotherapist contracted with a firm to destroy some obsolete records. The firm's shredder broke, so the individual doing the work took the remaining records home and put them in the fireplace to burn. The remains were then placed in the trash. However, because they were not completely destroyed, some clients could be identified along with some information. How responsible is the psychotherapist in what happened? (Refer to Appendix K for a possible answer.)

Professional Vignette C

A client who paid for services rendered decided to submit her receipts to an insurance company for reimbursement after nine months of therapy. The insurance company had the client sign a records release. When the psychotherapist informed the insurance company that he did not keep records, the insurance company refused to pay based on the concept that if it wasn't written down, it didn't occur. What are the possible consequences of this case?

CHAPTER 12

Conclusions and Frequently Asked Questions

Keeping Good Records

Good record keeping by you can be of value in facilitating treatment, improving psychotherapy skills, and managing your practice. In the event you are sued, carefully maintaining client records may mean the difference between a legal judgment for or against you as a service provider. If you have sloppy or sparse records, you are likely to appear unprofessional, uncaring, or deceptive. By maintaining complete records, you will appear competent. Also, your judgment is evaluated by the courts retrospectively. Thus, your records need to show that you made reasonable judgments based on the information available at the time. Record keeping need not be time consuming or cumbersome. However, it needs to show evidence that you took care in judgment, consulting with other clinicians when warranted, and that you assessed all risk factors concerning the client.

You are advised not to make cryptic or illegible notes. Moreover, avoid highly judgmental or derogatory statements. Furthermore, exercise care in correcting records. In litigation, such corrections may be seen as an attempt at "doctoring" the original record.

You need to limit the material entered into your client's records to what is necessary to advance treatment of the client. The type of record keeping needed is progress notes, as opposed to process notes. Clear descriptions, including behavioral observations, are advised. Hall (1988) may well have identified the problem in keeping records: "Apparently very little time is spent on this subject (records) in the typical education and training . . . of psychotherapists" (p. 3).

Maintaining Confidentiality

Perhaps the most important element in any psychotherapeutic relationship is the confidentiality of the communication. A client needs to feel that information transmitted to you will be protected in the course of treatment. Therefore, it is imperative that you discuss the limits of confidentiality before starting therapy. Stromberg et al. (1988, p. 387) suggest that you put in writing and inform your clients that they lose the right to a confidential relationship when any of the following occurs:

- They consent to disclosure.
- A law requires reporting an event.
- There is a duty to protect.
- Reimbursement requires disclosure.
- Legal rules require disclosure.
- They bring a lawsuit.
- An emergency exists.

Retention and Disposition of Records

Both professional guidelines and state laws mandate the retention of records. As there are significant differences among state laws, you must know your own state law to determine how long records need to be retained. Also, material in records can become obsolete. Therefore, before transferring or sending records elsewhere, review the material and identify which portions are no longer valid.

In disposing of records, the concept of confidentiality must be maintained. Moreover, it is best if you personally shred records. However, the task of disposing of records may be delegated or contracted for destruction. Also, burning or other destructive actions are acceptable. In any event, the responsibility for the destruction resides with you.

Some Final Tips

Here are some final thoughts that we recommend you follow:

- Document everything. (Remember the saying, "If it isn't written down, it didn't happen.")
- Inform your clients that they are free to withdraw the consent for treatment at any time.
- Inform your clients that they can obtain a second opinion, if desired.
- Inform your clients of the frequency, duration, and probable length of treatment.
- Discuss your fee, charges for phone consultations, missed appointments or late cancellations, and method of payment prior to the onset of treatment.
- Provide a statement that any questions the client has about therapeutic procedures will be answered at any time.
- Records are best kept in nonerasable black ink.
- Never erase. Cross out and write over or alter your notes.

Relevant Court Case

McMaster v. Iowa Board of Psychology Examiners
No. 354/92-1904 Iowa Supreme Court (1993)

Marsha McMaster was seen in psychotherapy by psychologist Todd Haines, and eventually they married. Marsha then started therapy with psychologist Susan Guenther. Following a complaint about alleged conduct between McMaster and Haines during their psychotherapist-patient relationship, the Iowa Board of Psychology sought Guenther's records without obtaining McMaster's permission.

Court Decision

A subpoena *duces tecum* was issued and the Iowa Supreme Court indicated that the Board of Psychology must prove that public interest outweighed the privacy interest. The high court outlined the following in rejecting the subpoena ordering Guenther to turn over the records:

1. The intrusion is justified because it furthers the investigation.
2. The records are necessary as evidence in connection with the disciplinary hearing.
3. The Board of Psychology must notify the client and try to obtain a release prior to issuing a subpoena.
4. The Board of Psychology must establish safeguards to prevent unauthorized disclosure of records.
5. The Board of Psychology needed to establish whether there is a statutory mandate, public policy, or recognized public interest in gaining access.

The Iowa Supreme Court *remanded* the case to permit the Board of Psychology to support its request for a subpoena.

Frequently Asked Questions

We are frequently asked the following questions by other psychotherapists and counselor trainees:

Question 1. Does it make a difference whether I write my progress notes during or after the therapy session?

Answer: No. Involve your clients. State your preference and get their okay.

Question 2. What is meant by "retroactive review of records" by insurance companies?

Answer: A retroactive review of your records is when they are later reviewed from the beginning to determine what you did and how the client responded (progressed).

Question 3. What should I do if a client tells me not to keep any records?

Answer: Indicate that it would be unprofessional not to keep records. Point out the advantages to the client.

Question 4. What should I do if my client asks to see the records I have on him?

Answer: Let him see his records. If you are afraid to do this, you might want to reevaluate how you keep records.

Question 5. What should I do if I receive a telephone call requesting release of records on one of my former clients?

Answer: First inform the requester that you cannot even acknowledge whether or not the alleged person was ever a client of yours. Second, tell the requester that you must have a written release that is signed by the supposed client, dated, and specifies the period of time for its effectiveness.

Question 6. What should I do if a client who has moved to another state requests that I send the file containing the original records?

Answer: The original file does not belong to the client. Not only can you explain this to your former client, you can ask the new therapist to explain it as well.

Question 7. Can I charge a fee for photocopying a client's records for the client?

Answer: Check your state as to the maximum you can charge per page. This issue is likely to be covered by a state law.

Question 8. What should I do if one of my clients is stalking me?

Answer: Consult with another psychotherapist and consider what action you might take, such as initiating a restraining order. Whatever action is taken is determined by the diagnosis.

Question 9. What should I do if a former client who has terminated therapy with me and has an outstanding balance requests a copy of his/her psychotherapy records? Can I withhold releasing the records until the balance is paid?

Answer: You can charge for photocopying, but you cannot withhold records because of an outstanding balance.

Question 10. Is the confidentiality of a client's record maintained after a client's death?

Answer: Yes. Even when a client dies, the therapist must still maintain confidentiality of the deceased client's records unless a personal representative signs a release for the information.

Question 11. If my licensing board takes legal action against me, can I be charged for the investigation and any prosecution expenses?

Answer: You need to refer to your respective state law. In California, the answer is "yes."

Question 12. If my licensing board takes legal action against me, are my legal fees covered by my malpractice insurance?

Answer: Not unless you have some special coverage for such an event.

Question 13. Could a psychotherapist have his or her license suspended for failure to disclose the fee to a prospective client?

Answer: In California, the answer is "yes." Psychotherapists in other states are governed by their state laws.

Question 14. How can a therapist record everything done in therapy?

Answer: It is impossible to write down everything. The therapist must determine what is significant.

Question 15. Record keeping takes time. Are there any ways to save time?

Answer: Eliminate unnecessary words. Review this book, especially the Case Record Example in Appendix B.

PART V

Appendixes

Appendix A

Legal Citations

Chapter 1: Protecting The Client and the Therapist

New York: *Whitree v. State of New York* (1968)
Michigan: *Detroit Edison v. National Labor Relations Board* (1979)
North Carolina: *White v. N.C. State Board of Examiners* (1990)
New York: *Susiovick v. New York State Education Department* (1991)
Michigan: *Detroit Edison v. National Labor Relations Board* (1979)

Chapter 2: Limits of Confidentiality

South Dakota: *Schaffer v. Spicer* (1974)
Illinois: *In re Donald Pebsworth Appeal of Dr. Kersey Anita* (1983)

Chapter 3: Contents of a Good Record

Diagnostic Error

Iowa: *Mrs. Kenneth Baker v. United State of America* (1964)
Alabama: *North American Company for Life and Health Insurance v. Berger* (1981)

Informed Consent

Alabama: *Underwood v. U.S.A.* (1966)
Michigan: *Stowers v. Wolodzko* (1971)

Treatment of a Minor

Illinois: *Dymek v. Nyquist* (1984)

Chapter 4: Families, Couples, and Group Psychotherapy

California: *Guity v. Kandilakis* (1991)
California: *James W. v. Superior Court* (1993)

Chapter 5: Supervision and Training

New York: *Cohen v. State of New York* (1975)

Chapter 6: Danger to Self

New York: *Willie Eady v. Jacob Alter* (1976)
California: *Bellah & Bellah v. Greenson* (1977)
California: *Johnson v. County of Los Angeles* (1983)

Chapter 7: Danger to Others

California: *Tarasoff v. The Regents of the University
   of California* (1975)
Maryland: *Shaw v. Glickman* (1980)
Nebraska: *Lipari & the Bank of Elkorn v. Sears Roebuck & Co
   & U.S.A.* (1980)
California: *Doyle and Doyle v. U.S.A.* (1982)
Minnesota: *Cairl et al. v. State of Minnesota et al.* (1982)
Michigan: *Davis v. Lhim* (1983)
Michigan: *Chrite v. U.S.A.* (1983)
District of Columbia: *White v. U.S.A.* (1986)
California: *People v. Kevin F.* (1989)
New York: *Oringer v. Rotkin* (1990)

Chapter 8: Abuse

Texas: *W.C.W. v. Bird* (1992)
Illinois: *Sullivan v. Cheshier* (1994)

Chapter 9: Treatment Of Minors

Wisconsin: *Wisconsin v. S. H.* (1990)

Chapter 10: Client Access To Records

California: *Cutter v. Brownbridge* (1986)
New York: *Jane Doe v. Joan Roe & Peter Poe* (1977)
Indiana: *Watters v. Dinn* (1994)

Chapter 11: Retention And Disposition Of Records

New York: *Estate of Finkle* (1977)

Chapter 12: Conclusions And Frequently Asked Questions

Iowa: *McMaster v. Iowa Board of Psychology Examiners* (1993)

Appendix B

Case Record Example

EXAMPLE	ANN	Elaine	F			14.2	8-16-80
Last Name	First Name	Middle	Sex	S M W D		Age	Citizenship

Lakeview Lane #10034		Anywhere	00001-XXXX	(909) 000-0001
Residence address		City	Zip	Home Telephone

Student	Lovely H.S.	Anywhere	(909) 000-0002
Occupation	Employed at or Business	Address	Work Telephone

Example, Bob	Yes(when in the US)	Overseas Oil United	Iran	DK
Name of (father)	Living with Client	Employed at or Business	Address	Work Telephone

Example, Mary	Yes	Lawyer's Company	Somewhere (909) 001-1111
Name of (mother)	Living with Client	Employed at or Business	Address Work Telephone

No Insurance	-	Mother Will Pay Each Session	Both mother & father
Type of CPS or Group Insurance Coverage			Custody of Client

Mother - Mary	Mary Example	Same as Ann
Referred by	Render bill to	Address & Phone

SS# 000-00-0000	SS# 555-555-555
Social Security Number of Client	Social Security Number of parent

Date	Progress	Fee

10-28-94   Split session (1st half with Mary - 2nd half with Ann)
#100.00(paid)

_____ History from Mother (Mary):

_____ **CHIEF COMPLAINT**: "Ann started ditching school this year.

_____ Ann has always been A-B student & now is C-D." Also, she

_____ is moody, i.e., "cries a lot". **HISTORY:** Born at Kaiser Hospital

_____ (Fontana). Raised in So. CA. Father (Bob) is oilfield worker in

_____ Iran. "He works overseas for 18 mos. at a time then comes home

_____ for 30-45 days. He just went back at middle of Sept." Age-40

_____ Mother (Mary) has been going to college - received MA in Hosp.

_____ Admin. and started work Sept. 20th this year. Age-39. Sibs -

_____ None. Note: Mother went to sch. & then worked because she

_____ was "bored at home". CONTINUED

150

Date	Progress	Fee

10-28-94   **SCHOOL:** Ann started 9th grade this year. "Always an A-B

student". Note: Mary will mail or bring in some prior Report Cards.

"Ann loves to read". She has no specific goals for future. "Some

talk of becoming a writer".

HEALTH: (5'5"/115 lbs.) "Excellent" Had physical exam at

beginning of sch. year. **BIRTH & DEVELOPMENT:** "Normal"

No serious ill. or impair. requiring hospitalization. No known use of

drugs/alcohol. No suicide threats or attempts. No history

of psychotherapy.

HISTORY FROM ANN:

Chief Complaint: Knows her grades have gone down as the

result of truancy and not doing homework. Does not want to fail as

she "wants to go to college". Relates that she "broke up with boy-

friend the week before her Father left for overseas." Then her mom

went to work. "I have no one to talk to". Confirmed no drugs or

alcohol. Although she has been "unhappy" past 2 mos., she denied

any suicidal ideation. She likes reading - seldom watches TV. Would

like to be a writer (books).

ˏOriented X 3 .

3 wishes: 1) Be a writer

2) Have boyfriend back

3) Have both mother and father home

See mother/dad together on 11-4-94.   **s/Dr. XYZ**

Date	Progress	Fee

11-2-94   Phone Note: Mother called to indicate that she couldn't find any REPORT
           CARDS. Told her we would discuss on 11-4-94.

11-24-94   Phone Note: Mother called to let me know that teachers have all
           reported "MARKED IMPROVEMENT   in grades, attendance &
           attitude".   OK to discuss with Ann.

           TERMINATION SUMMARY:
           AFTER TOTAL OF 8 SESSIONS this case was closed by mutual
           agreement of therapist, Ann & her mother. Throughout therapy Ann did
           not ditch school once reflecting a 100% achievement of Behavioral
           Objective. Also, her semester grades were 3 A's & 3 B's again
           resulting in 100% Behavioral Objective obtained.
           EXCELLENT PROGNOSIS

Appendix C

Progress Notes Example

Name: __ANN Example__   Date: __2-7-95__   15 __30__ 45 __60__

Individual: __X__   Canceled: _____ Emerg. _____ Office: __X__

Couple: ____   Late Can. ____   Failed: ____   Hosp.

Family: ____   On Time: __X__   Late: ____   Other:

Group:

Observations/Appearance/Affect: __Excellent mood & Appearance. Brought in__

__mother.__

Content/Topics: __Termination issues. More re: 1) New boyfriend, 2) Mother's__

__increased communication & involvement.__

Significant/Recent Events: __"Got 3 A's & 3 B's for semester grades"__

__* EXCELLENT PROGNOSIS.__

Assignments/Homework:

Diagnosis: __309.4__ _____ Tentative New Same

Treatment Plan: Continued New Replaced   **Referral:**   Medical:

Suicide: Yes   No   Psychiatric:

Violence: Yes   No   Neurological:

Next session: __CASE CLOSED__ _____ **Signature:** __s/Dr. XYZ__

153

Name: ANN Example   Date: 1-4-95   15___30___45_X_60

Individual: X   Canceled: Emerg.   Office: X
Couple: ___   Late Can. ___   Failed: ___   Hosp.
Family: ___   On Time: X   Late: ___   Other:
Group:

Observations/Appearance/Affect: Excellent mood & Appearance. Brought in

 by mother.

Content/Topics: "I have a new boyfriend" "Everything going well" "Don't think I

need to see you anymore" Semester ends 2-3-95.

Significant/Recent Events: *"Mom spent a lot of time with me during vacation. We

talked like we use to". • Introduction to TERMINATION ISSUES.

Assignments/Homework: Knows she can call if needs to before her last session

scheduled for Feb. 7th

Diagnosis: 309.4 _____ Tentative New Same

Treatment Plan: Continued New Replaced   **Referral:** Medical
Suicide: Yes No   Psychiatric
Violence: Yes No   Neurological

Next session: 2-7-95 _____   **Signature:** s/Dr. XYZ _____

PROGRESS NOTES

Name:__ANN Example_____ Date:____11-30-94_____ 15 X _30 ___45 ___60

Individual:	Canceled: _X_	Emerg.	Office:
Couple: ___	Late Can. ___	Failed: ___	Hosp.
Family: ___	On Time: ___	Late: ___	Other: Phone
Group:			NO CHARGE

Observations/Appearance/Affect:

Content/Topics:

Significant/Recent Events: _Maternal Grandfather died - went East - Will be gone

until 12-7-94 - Rescheduled 12-13-94._

Assignments/Homework:

Diagnosis:_____ Tentative New Same

Treatment Plan: Continued New Replaced   Referral: Medical
Suicide: Yes No   Psychiatric
Violence: Yes No   Neurological

Next session:__12-13-94_____ Signature:__s/Dr.__

XYZ_____

Name:__ANN Example_____ Date:____12-13-94_____ 15 ___30 ___45 ___60

Individual: _X_	Canceled: _____	Emerg.	Office: _X_
Couple: ___	Late Can. ___	Failed: ___	Hosp.
Family: ___	On Time: _X_	Late: ___	Other:
Group:			

Observations/Appearance/Affect:__Brought in by Aunt as Mother was working.
Excellent appearance cont. but appeared Sad.

Content/Topics: Discussed my Vacation plans - Will not see until 1/95 "O.K." "I
won't be in school those 2 weeks anyway". Discussed Grandfather's death - more
hypnosis

Significant/Recent Events: * Therapist on Vacation last 2 weeks - December

Assignments/Homework:_Cont. doing homework. - Has term paper to do in 2 classes.
Contracted to work on during 2 week vacation.

Diagnosis: 309.4_____ Tentative New Same

Treatment Plan: Continued New Replaced   Referral: Medical:
Suicide: Yes No   Psychiatric:
Violence: Yes No   Neurological:

Next session: 1-4-95   **Signature:** s/Dr. XYZ

PROGRESS NOTES

Name: ___ANN Example_____ Date:___11-18-94_____ 15___30___45_X__60

Individual: _X_____ Canceled: _____ Emerg. _____ Office:_X
Couple: _____ Late Can. ____ Failed: ____ Hosp.
Family: _____ On Time: _X___ Late: _____ Other:
Group:

Observations/Appearance/Affect: _Brought in by Aunt as Mother working._ Noted improvement in Mood.

Content/Topics: _"Didn't feel like ditching once past week"_ "Enjoyed doing my homework" DISCUSSED TEST RESULTS - Hypnosis

Significant/Recent Events: *Wrote story for English & got A+. Note: IQ in 95%ile & Achievement, all above grade level.

Assignments/Homework: ___Cont. to do homework daily_____

Diagnosis: 309.4 _____ Tentative New Same

Treatment Plan: Continued New Replaced   Referral: Medical
Suicide: Yes No   Psychiatric
Violence: Yes No   Neurological

Next session: _11-25-94_____ **Signature:** ___s/ Dr. XYZ_____

Name:___ANN Example_____ Date:___11-25-94_____ 15___30___45___60

Individual: _X_____ Canceled: _____ Emerg. _____ Office:_X
Couple: _____ Late Can. ____ Failed: ____ Hosp.
Family: _____ On Time: _X___ Late: _____ Other:
Group:

Observations/Appearance/Affect: _Brought in by Mother - Excellent mood & Appearance._ Cont. to be spontaneous.

Content/Topics: _Brought in story she wrote for me to read. Another week of no desire to ditch. Also, enjoys homework. Gave her positive feedback re: teacher reports._

Significant/Recent Events: _Used hypnosis again_

Assignments/Homework: ___Cont. to do homework daily_

Diagnosis: 309.4 _____ Tentative New Same

Treatment Plan: Continued New Replaced   Referral: Medical:
Suicide: Yes No   Psychiatric:
Violence: Yes No   Neurological:

Next session: _12-1-94_____ **Signature:** ___s/ Dr. XYZ__

PROGRESS NOTES

Name: ANN Example   **Date:** 11-4-94   15___ 30___ 45 X 60

Individual: _____ Canceled: _____ Emerg. _____ Office: X
Couple: ___ Late Can. ___ Failed: ___ Hosp. ___
Family: _X_ On Time: __X__ Late: ___ Other: ___
Group:

Observations/Appearance/Affect: Mother and Dad seen together.

Content/Topics: Discussed: 1) Informed Consent, 2) Limits of Confidentiality, 3) Made out Treatment Plan together, 4) Testing for IQ & Achievement.

Significant/Recent Events: * Mother understands she will pay psychologist for testing. She will schedule ASAP.

Assignments/Homework: Ann will not ditch school during the next week & will do 1hr. homework each day.

Diagnosis: 309.4 Adjustment Reaction with mixed dist. _____ Tentative New Same

Treatment Plan: Continued New Replaced   **Referral:** Medical
Suicide: Yes No   Psychiatric
Violence: Yes No   Neurological

Next session: 11-9-94 _____   **Signature:** s/Dr. XYZ

Name: ANN Example   **Date:** 11-9-94   15___ 30___ 45 X 60

Individual: X _____ Canceled: _____ Emerg. _____ Office: X
Couple: ___ Late Can. ___ Failed: ___ Hosp. ___
Family: ___ On Time: _X_ Late: ___ Other: ___
Group:

Observations/Appearance/Affect: Brought to therapy by Mother. Excellent appearance - Spontaneous verbalization

Content/Topics: Utilized hypnosis - Excellent response. "Only felt like ditching 3X's last week but didn't - It was hard not to".

Significant/Recent Events: * IQ & Achievement Testing with Dr. Know - set for 11-4-94.

Assignments/Homework: Cont. doing homework daily. - She will control amount of time. Also, no truancy.

Diagnosis: 309.4 _____ Tentative New Same

Treatment Plan: Continued New Replaced   **Referral:** Medical:
Suicide: Yes No   Psychiatric:
Violence: Yes No   Neurological:

Next session: 11-18-94 _____   **Signature:** s/Dr. XYZ

Appendix D

Treatment Plan

Name: Ann Example
11-4-94

Problem Area:

1. School attendance and homework
2. School grades
3.
4.

Behavioral Objective:	*Time Frame:*
1. Decrease truancy by 75%	1. 3 months
2. Improve all grades to B or A	2. 3 months
3.	3.
4.	4.

Concepts/skills to Develop:

1. Develop good study habits
2. Focus on significance of grades in getting into college
3.
4.

Materials/Activities:

1. Hypnosis: (a) suggestions to improve memory, (b) improve attendance, and (c) improve homework
2. Verbal-directive psychotherapy—Reality-oriented therapy
3.
4.

Appendix E

Billing for Services

CASE NAME:_____ANN EXAMPLE_____

BILLING INFORMATION:_____MARY EXAMPLE_____

_____10034 Lakeview Lane_____

_____Anywhere, CA   00001_____

_____$100.00 Session_____

Date	Function	Time	Charge	Paid
10-28-94	Individual Psychotherapy (History)	50 min.	100.00	100.00
11-4-94	Psychotherapy (Mother/Father)	50 min.	100.00	100.00
11-9-94	Individual Psychotherapy	45 min.	100.00	100.00
11-18-94	Individual Psychotherapy	45 min.	100.00	100.00
11-25-94	Individual Psychotherapy	45 min.	100.00	100.00
12-13-94	Individual Psychotherapy	45 min.	100.00	100.00
1-4-95	Individual Psychotherapy	45 min.	100.00	100.00
2-7-95	Individual Psychotherapy	45 min.	100.00	100.00
			CASE CLOSED	

159

Appendix F

Informed Consent

I (we), **Mary and Ann Example**, assert that I have discussed the goals, objectives, methods, and time frame of my Treatment Plan with my psychotherapist **Dr. XYZ**. I understand that the above may be modified as therapy progresses. I understand that I have the right to refuse treatment or to terminate psychotherapy should I choose. I understand fully the risks, alternatives, and the nature of the treatment to be employed. I am aware that my psychotherapist will discuss these or any other issues should I request. At this time, I consent to work toward the achievement of the objectives stated in my Treatment Plan. I further specifically limit my therapist's use of any information which can in any way identify me to others unless I have offered my specific written permission. It is without any pressure or coercion that I sign this consent.

I agree to compensate my therapist at the rate of $100.00 per *each* session.

Date: 10-28-94 _____

Signature: s/Mary Example s/Ann Example _____

Witness: s/Miss Observant _____

Appendix G

Consent Form for Audio/Video Recording

Agreement entered into this _____day of_____between

Dr._____Whereas,

Dr._____is desirous of using videotape and/or audiotape for the purpose of professional education, treatment and research, and is desirous of endorsing and supporting the use of such videotape, for the purpose of professional education treatment and research. It is agreed by both parties hereto as follows:

1. The client consents to the use of videotape, and/or audiotape hereinafter to be taken in the office of Dr._____ during the course of individual treatment.

2. The said videotape and/or audiotape will be used solely in the interest of the advancement of mental health programs and only for the purpose of professional education, treatment or research activities connected with the programs, and will not be used for any other purpose.

3. Dr. _____agrees not to use or permit the use of the name of _____in connection with any direct or indirect use of exhibition of such videotape and/or audiotape.

4. I agree that Dr._____is the sole owner of all rights in and to the said videotape and/or audiotape for all purposes herein set forth.

5. There shall be no financial compensation for the use of such videotape and/or audiotape.

_____ Date
Psychotherapist

_____ Date
Patient

_____ Date
Witness

161

Appendix H

Fax Cover Letter Consent Form

PLEASE DELIVER THE FOLLOWING RIGHT AWAY TO:

Name: _____

Firm: _____

FAX   NO: _____

From: _____

Date: _____

Reference: _____

TOTAL PAGES INCLUDING COVER PAGE. IF YOU DO NOT RECEIVE
ALL THE PAGES, PLEASE PHONE AS SOON AS POSSIBLE AT ( ) _____

******************CONFIDENTIAL TRANSMISSION************************
The accompanying documents contain confidential or legally privileged
information transmitted by _____. This information is
only for the use of the person named on this transmission sheet. If you
are not the intended recipient, you are not authorized to use, disclose or
copy any of the information and you should promptly notify _____
by telephone ( ) _____ of the erroneous transmission so arrangements
for the return of the documents can be made at our expense.

Appendix I

California
Limitation on Confidentiality:
A Brochure for Clients

We greatly respect your right of privacy especially regarding information you share in therapy. We also believe you should fully understand the limitations of confidentiality in order for you to make an informed decision regarding what you disclose in therapy.

We are required to disclose confidential information to regulated third parties if any of the following conditions exist:

(01) You are a danger to yourself or others.

(02) You seek treatment to and/or enable anyone to commit a crime or to avoid detection or apprehension.

(03) Your therapist was appointed by the court to evaluate you.

(04) Your contact with your therapist is for the purpose of determining sanity in a criminal proceeding.

(05) Your contact is part of a proceeding to establish your competence.

(06) The contact is one in which your psychotherapist must file a report to a public employee or as information required to be recorded in a public office, if such report or record is open to public inspection.

(07) You are under 16 years old, and you are the victim of a crime.

(08) You are a minor, and your psychotherapist reasonably suspects you are a victim of child abuse.

(09) You are a person over age 65, and your psychotherapist believes you are the victim of physical abuse; your therapist may disclose information if you are the victim of emotional abuse.

(10) You die, and the communication is important to decide an issue concerning a deed of conveyance, will, or other writing executed by you affecting an interest in property.

(11) You die, and the communication is important as to your intent related to a deed of conveyance, will, or other writing executed by you.

(12) You file suit against your therapist for breach of a duty or if your therapist files suit against you.

(13) The communication is important to an issue between parties claiming through you after you have died.

(14) You have filed suit against anyone and have claimed mental/ emotional damages, as a part of the suit.

(15) You waive your right to privilege or give consent to limited disclosure by your therapist.

(16) If you fail to pay your bill, your psychotherapist may turn your case over for collection.

Appendix J

California's Consent and Disclosure Requirements for Minors

If the Patient Is Under 18 Years of Age	Whose Consent Is Required for Care?	Can Parents Be Notified of Care?
A. There are no other special circumstances	Parent/Legal guardian	Yes
B. (Implied Consent) There is an emergency and the parents cannot be contacted	No one need consent	Yes
C. (Transfer of Consent Power) There is a document signed	Person named in document by a parent transferring consent power	Yes
D. (Totally Emancipated)		
1. Is or has ever been legally married	Minor	Not unless minor agrees
2. Is on active military duty	Minor	Not unless minor agrees
3. Is over 15, not living at home and managing own financial affairs	Minor	Not unless minor agrees
4. Has an ID card from DMV stating emancipated minor	Minor	Not unless minor agrees
E. (Partially Emancipated)		
1. If 12 years or older, is in need of outpatient mental health care, is a danger to self, and/or to others, and may be a victim of child abuse	Minor, for outpatient mental health care	Involvement of parent if required unless physician decides notification is not appropriate
2. Is 12 years or older and has a drug- or alcohol-related problem	Minor, for the drug or alcohol problems	Same as above
3. Is alleged to have been sexually assaulted	Minor, for care of sexual assault	Yes, if the parent is not responsible for the sexual assault

165

Appendix K

Answers to Vignettes Presented in Chapters

Chapter 1: Protecting the Client and the Therapist (Vignette B, page 18)

This is one way of dealing with a subpoena for original material, as you need to be able to retain your "tools of the trade." Should an issue arise regarding photocopying of copyright materials, it would be wise to contact the holder of the copyright, who might want to have their attorney fight for the protection of that copyright. Also, consider contacting the American Psychological Association, who might wish to enter the picture to protect the tests in question owing to the probable loss of reliability.

Chapter 2: Limits of Confidentiality (Vignette, page 28)

You do not make a child abuse report based on this meager information, for "thinks it must be her father's hand" and that "he probably sexually abused her" are too vague. You need more information, For example, what makes her "think" so, and what does she mean by "probably"? At what age?—when she was younger? Where did it happen? Responses to these questions would help clarify the picture.

Chapter 3: Contents of a Good Record (Vignette G, page 55)

Any case in which a psychotherapist is having a problem with a client is an excellent occasion to consult another therapist. If the consultant does nothing more than support/confirm your treatment plan, it at least lets you know you are on a solid foundation. Frequently, however, the consultant will open up new ideas, thoughts, approaches, and so on that gives the therapist new alternatives. Of course, any consultations should be documented.

Chapter 4: Families, Couples, and Group
Psychotherapy (Vignette A, page 61)

A person can only consent to the release of his or her own records. If you kept separate records, you would send only the wife's. If you did not keep separate records, you would have to (a) omit parts that the husband holds are confidential, (b) receive the husband's consent to release his records, and (c) be aware that the judge could order you to release the husband's records. (If this occurs, you can ask the judge to review the file "in camera" [chambers] to determine what needs to be released.)

Chapter 5: Supervision and Training (Vignette A, page 68)

This vignette highlights the issue of confidentiality, which needs to be explored in the first session when one is seeing an individual, couple, or family. If a therapist's policy is not to guarantee confidentiality when seeing one partner alone, this needs to be stated from the outset. However, if this is not the policy and a therapist is willing to keep confidentiality when seeing one spouse alone, we suggest that at that time it is best to keep a separate record. Records need to reflect what the rules are concerning the issue of confidentiality. For example, we suggest that you keep a separate file on the husband who has tested HIV positive and maintain another file on the couple. This we believe is especially warranted if you had explained to the couple that you would keep in confidence any conversations you had with them alone.

Another point brought forth by this vignette is the matter of privileged information. That is, who can have access to records, and under what conditions? In this case, the wife's lawyer cannot obtain records that contain data about her husband without his written consent. Nor could you send records, even to her lawyer, that contain data about her without her written consent. If the husband did not give his signed consent for his wife to have access to their records, we suggest that you contact her lawyer and explain your inability to obtain consent and grant their request. Of course, the judge can request their records without consent, and you must then comply.

If you do keep separate records, the outcome could be different because the husband might be more agreeable to having their joint record sent to his wife's lawyer. He could be assured that the issue he is most concerned about her knowing (HIV) would not be made public.

Finally, we suggest that there is an alternative to sending an entire copy of a file, and that is to write a summary statement regarding their treatment. This could be a one-page writeup containing information you believe would be appropriate considering the circumstance. We suggest the husband and wife be given a copy (of the summary statement) prior to receiving their signed consent.

Chapter 6: Danger to Self (Vignette A, page 82)

One possible suggestion is to ask the husband if he knows what set her off—for example, did they have a fight? This is information not obtained from your client. You have not talked to her or observed her and do not know about the reliability of the information presented. Therefore, you might advise the husband to call the police and seek their assistance in finding his wife and getting her evaluated. You record the information the husband gives you and what you advised him to do.

Chapter 7: Danger to Others (Vignette, page 101)

Be aware that there is a difference between "thoughts" and "actions." You must determine if her thoughts are only an expression of her anger *or* an intent to kill him. Your questions must be designed to determine if she has actually made a threat or shown intent to kill him. If so, it is a mandated report in some states, such as California, where the therapist must notify both law enforcement and the husband (don't assume he knows). If no threat is made, you evaluate the need for her hospitalization as a possible danger to others, write what you did, and state both the time and the name notified.

Chapter 8: Abuse (Vignette, page 109)

If this 16-year-old is emancipated, she is legally considered an adult. Thus, you would not release records to her mother unless the 16-year-old authorized you to do so. Because her father is serving time in prison for the abuse, your patient may have no objections regarding signing a release. If so, it is suggested you discuss a release to send the mother a summary report as opposed to a photocopy of the records. Document what transpired and any specific release given and signed by your client.

Chapter 9: Treatment of Minors (Vignette, page 119)

You must know your state law. For example, in California you can see a minor aged 12 or older who is involved with drugs without parental consent. It is your choice. Consider whether he can pay or if you are willing to do this for free. If you try to use the parents' insurance, the parents will most likely find out. Also, consider that you would most likely end up in court due to the child custody issue. Document as though you know your record will be part of the court proceeding. This also is an excellent case to seek consultation (and, of course, document this in the record).

Chapter 10: Client Access to Records (Vignette, page 131)

If the state has no law regarding client access to records, you must refer to your professional code of ethics. Peer consultation would be appropriate and, of course, documented. It would also be wise to consult with legal counsel.

Chapter 11: Retention and Disposition of Records (Vignette B, page 138)

The psychotherapist is responsible for the destruction of records. Although an outside firm can be retained to perform this service, it is a good idea to contract with a reputable firm that is bonded and insured.

Appendix L

Ethical Codes Related to Record Keeping

The specific ethical guidelines pertaining to record keeping among six of the mental health professions are as follows:

- American Association for Marriage and Family Therapy (1991) *AAMFT Code of Ethics*

   2.3. Marriage and family therapists store or dispose of client records in ways that maintain confidentiality.

- American Counseling Association (1995) *Code of Ethics and Standards of Practice*

   B.4. Records

   a. *Requirement of Records.* Counselors maintain records necessary for rendering professional services to their clients and as required by laws, regulations, or agency or institution procedures.

   b. *Confidentiality of Records.* Counselors are responsible for securing the safety and confidentiality of any counseling records they create, maintain, transfer, or destroy whether the records are written, taped, computerized, or stored in any other medium. (See B.1.a.)

   c. *Permission to Record or Observe.* Counselors obtain permission from clients prior to electronically recording or observing sessions. (See A.3.a.)

   d. *Client Access.* Counselors recognize that counseling records are kept for the benefit of clients and therefore provide access to records and copies of records when requested by competent clients, unless the records contain information that may be misleading and detrimental to the client. In situations involving multiple clients, access to records is limited to those parts of records that do not include confidential information related to another client. (See A.8., B.1.a., and B.2.b.)

e. *Disclosure or Transfer.* Counselors obtain written permission from clients to disclose or transfer records to legitimate third parties unless exceptions to confidentiality exist as listed in Section B.1. Steps are taken to ensure that receivers of counseling records are sensitive to their confidential nature.

■ American Psychiatric Association (1986)
Principles of Medical Ethics, with Annotations Especially Applicable to Psychiatry

4.1. Psychiatric records, including even the identification of a person as a patient, must be protected with extreme care. Confidentiality is essential to psychiatric treatment. This is based in part on the special nature of psychiatric therapy as well as on the traditional ethical relationship between physician and patient. Growing concern regarding civil rights of patients and the possible adverse effects of computerization, duplication equipment, and data banks makes the dissemination of confidential information an increasing hazard. Because of the sensitive and private nature of the information with which the psychiatrist deals, he/she must be circumspect in the information that he/she chooses to disclose to others about a patient. The welfare of the patient must be a continuing consideration.

4.2. A psychiatrist may release confidential information only with the authorization of the patient or under proper legal compulsion. The continuing duty of the psychiatrist to protect the patient includes fully apprising him/her of the connotations of waiving the privilege of privacy. This may become an issue when the patient is being investigated by a government agency, is applying for a position, or is involved in a legal action. The same principles apply to the release of information concerning treatment to medical departments of government agencies, business organizations, labor unions, and insurance companies. Information gained in confidence about patients seen in student health services should not be released without the student's explicit permission.

4.5. Ethically, the psychiatrist may disclose only that
information which is relevant to a given situation. He/she
should avoid offering speculation as fact. Sensitive information such as an individual's sexual orientation or fantasy
material is usually considered unnecessary.

■ American Psychological Association (1992)
Ethical Principles of Psychologists and Code of Conduct
1.24   Records and Data
Psychologists create, maintain, disseminate, store, retain, and
dispose of records and data relating to their research,
practice, and other work in accordance with law and in a
manner that permits compliance with the requirements of
this Ethics Code.
5.04   Maintenance of Records
Psychologists maintain appropriate confidentiality in
creating, storing, accessing, transferring, and disposing of
records under their control, whether these are written, auto-
mated, or in any other medium. Psychologists maintain and
dispose of records in accordance with law and in a manner
that permits compliance with the requirements of this Ethics
Code.

■ Association for Specialists in Group Work (1989)
Ethical Guidelines for Group Counselors
3. (e) Group counselors video- or audiotape a group session
only with prior consent, and the member's knowledge of
how the tape will be used.
3. (h) Group counselors store or dispose of group member
records (written, audio, video, etc.) in ways that maintain
confidentiality.

■ National Association of Social Workers (1996)
Code of Ethics
1.08   Access to Records
a. Social workers should provide clients with reasonable
access to records concerning the clients. Social workers
who are concerned that clients' access to their records
could cause serious misunderstanding or harm to the client

should provide assistance in interpreting the records and consultation with the client regarding the records. Social workers should limit clients' access to their records, or portions of their records, only in exceptional circumstances when there is compelling evidence that such access would cause serious harm to the client. Both clients' requests and the rationale for withholding some or all of the record should be documented in clients' files.

b. When providing clients with access to their records, social workers should take steps to protect the confidentiality of other individuals identified or discussed in such records.

3.04 Client Records

a. Social workers should take reasonable steps to ensure that documentation in records is accurate and reflects the services provided.

b. Social workers should include sufficient and timely documentation in records to facilitate the delivery of services and to ensure continuity of services provided to clients in the future.

c. Social workers' documentation should protect clients' privacy to the extent that is possible and appropriate and should include only information that is directly relevant to the delivery of services.

d. Social workers should store records following the termination of services to ensure reasonable future access. Records should be maintained for the number of years required by state statutes or relevant contracts.

Appendix M

Glossary of Legal Terms Pertaining to Psychotherapy

- **Confidential communication**—This includes "information obtained by an examination of the patient, transmitted between a patient and his psychotherapist in the course of that relationship and in confidence . . . and includes a diagnosis made and the advice given by the psychotherapist in the course of the relationship" (Evidence Code 1012). A client or other party who hold the privilege has the right, except in certain legally defined situations, to protect confidential communications from being revealed in legal proceedings.

- **Confidentiality**—This refers to an ethical responsibility that protects clients from unauthorized disclosure of information given in confidence to a mental health professional. Although confidentiality is primarily an ethical responsibility, several state laws (including California) stipulate that a psychotherapist may lose his or her license for willful, unauthorized communication of information received in professional confidence. Also, a number of state laws (including California) either mandate or permit breaches of confidentiality in certain situations.

- **Emancipated minor**—This is a minor who is free from the legal authority of parents or guardians. Under California law, a minor who is at least age 14 may become emancipated by marrying legally, enlisting in the military, or by meeting certain legally defined requirements and filing a petition with the court. Emancipated minors are treated legally as if they were adults and thus can consent to medical and psychological treatment.

- **Health care provider**—This means any of the following: (1) a licensed health facility, (2) a licensed clinic, (3) a licensed home health agency, (4) a licensed physician/surgeon, (5) a licensed podiatrist, (6) a licensed dentist, (7) a licensed psychologist, (8) a licensed optometrist, (9) a licensed chiropractor, (10) a licensed marriage, family, and child counselor, and (11) a licensed clinical social worker (Health and Safety Code 123105).

- **Mental health records**—These are patient records relating to evaluation or treatment of a mental disorder. These records include, but are not limited to, substance abuse (drugs and/or alcohol) records (Health and Safety Code 123105).

- **Minor**—In California, this means an individual under the age of 18 who has not been emancipated.

- **Patient**—This refers to a person who consults a psychotherapist for the purpose of diagnosis and/or treatment of an emotional condition (Evidence Code 1011).

- **Patient records**—These are records in any form or medium maintained by or in the custody of a health care provider relating to the patient's health history, diagnosis, and treatment provided to the patient. Patient records do not include information given in confidence by a person other than another health care provider or the patient and such material may be removed from the record prior to inspection or copying (Health and Safety Code 123105).

- **Privilege**—This is a legal term that refers to an individual's right to not have confidential information revealed in court or other legal proceedings without permission.

  Holder of the privilege—the person who has the right to waive the privilege, which is the right not to have confidential information revealed in legal proceedings. The "holder of the privilege" is (1) the client when he has no guardian or conservator, (2) the guardian or conservator when there is one, and (3) a personal representative of the client if the client is dead (Evidence Code 1013). The psychotherapist should claim the privilege (i.e., to assert the right) for the client unless disclosure is instructed by the person authorized to permit disclosure (Evidence Code 1015).

  Exceptions to privilege—refers to situations in which an individual does not have the right to prevent confidential information from being revealed in court or legal proceedings. Some of these exceptions also detail situations in which a psychotherapist is legally permitted but not mandated to breach confidentiality. Below are listed some of the exceptions to privilege:

  (a) **Patient-litigant exception**—exists when there is a relevant issue concerning the mental or emotional condition of the client (Evidence Code 1016).

  (b) **Court-appointed psychotherapist exception**—exists when a psychotherapist is appointed pursuant to court order to examine the patient. "This exception does not apply where the court has appointed a psychotherapist at the request of defendant's lawyer in a criminal proceeding for the purpose of determining whether defendant should enter a plea based on insanity or base a defense on his or her mental or emotional condition" (Evidence Code 1017).

(c) **Crime or tort exception**—when the services of the psychotherapist were sought to aid in the commitment of a crime or tort or to escape detection or apprehension following the commission of a crime or tort (Evidence Code 1018).

(d) **Deceased patient exception**—exists when personal representative of the client authorizes or whenever claims are made, regardless of testate of intestate (Evidence Code 1019).

(e) **Breach of duty arising out of the psychotherapist-patient relationship**—eliminates the privilege. The issue of breach (i.e., violation or breaking of a contractual agreement between two persons) can be by the therapist or by the client (Evidence Code 1020).

(f) **Proceeding to determine sanity of criminal defendant**—when initiated at the request of the defendant in a criminal action to determine his/her sanity results in no privilege (Evidence Code 1023).

(g) **Patient dangerous to self or others**—eliminates privilege if the psychotherapist has reasonable cause to believe the patient is in a mental or emotional condition that causes him or her to be dangerous to self, others, or property of another. Disclosure of the communication is necessary to prevent the threatened danger (Evidence Code 1024).

(h) **Proceeding to establish competence**—results in no privilege (Evidence Code 1025).

(i) **Required report**—which is open to the public, when information is required by a public employee or to be recorded in a public office, results in no privilege (Evidence Code 1026).

- **Psychotherapist**—This is a person who is authorized or believed by the patient to be authorized to practice psychotherapy. In California, this would be a licensed individual such as a psychologist, psychiatrist, marriage counselor, clinical social worker, intern, or psychological assistant (Evidence Code 1010).

- **Psychotherapist-patient privilege**—The relationship beween psychotherapist and patient is one that has been viewed as special and unique. To encourage a free and unrestrained exchange of communication between a psychotherapist and his or her patient, society has sought to protect this exchange from being disclosed to anyone. The patient can prevent disclosure to third parties except under very narrow exceptions (Evidence Code 1014).

- **Psychotherapy**—As defined by the laws of the state of California, psychotherapy is defined as "the use of psychological methods in a professional relationship to assist a person or persons to acquire greater human effectiveness or to modify feelings, conditions, attitudes, and behaviors which are emotionally, intellectually, or socially ineffectual or maladjustive."

- **Subpoena**—This is a written legal order requiring a person to appear in court to testify and/or produce certain written records.

References

Ahia, C. E., & Martin, D. (1993). *The danger-to-self-or-others exception to confidentiality* (ACA Legal Series, Vol. 8). Alexandria, VA: American Counseling Association.

American Association for Marriage and Family Therapy. (1991). *AAMFT code of ethics.* Washington, DC: Author.

American Counseling Association. (1995). *Code of ethics and standards of practice.* Alexandria, VA: Author.

American Psychiatric Association. (1989). *Principles of medical ethics, with annotations especially applicable to psychiatry.* Washington, DC: Author.

American Psychological Association. (1981). Specialty guidelines for the delivery of services by clinical psychologists. *American Psychologist, 36,* 640-651.

American Psychological Association. (1982). *Ethical principles in the conduct of research with human participants.* Washington, DC: Author.

American Psychological Association. (1987). General guidelines for providers of psychological services. *American Psychologist, 42,* 712-723.

American Psychological Association. (1992). Ethical principles of psychologists and code of conduct. *American Psychologist, 47,* 1597-1611.

Appelbaum, P. S. (1985). Tarasoff and the clinician: Problems in fulfilling the duty to protect. *American Journal of Psychiatry, 142,* 425-429.

Austin, K. M., Moline, M. E., & Williams, G. T. (1990). *Confronting malpractice: Legal and ethical dilemmas in psychotherapy.* Newbury Park, CA: Sage.

Bennett, B. E., Bryant, B. K., VandenBos, G. R., & Greenwood, A. (1990). *Professional liability and risk management.* Washington, DC: American Psychological Association.

Berger, M. (1982). Ethics and the therapeutic relationship: Patient rights and therapist responsibilities. In Rosenbaum, M. (Ed.), *Ethics and values in psychotherapy: A guidebook* (pp. 67-95). New York: Free Press.

Bergin, A. E., & Lambert, M. J. (1978). The evaluation of therapeutic outcome. In A. E. Bergin & S. L. Garfield (Eds.), *Handbook of psychotherapy and behavior change: An empirical analysis* (2nd ed.). New York: John Wiley.

Bursley, K. A. (April 6, 1988). [Letter to the California State Psychological Association].

CAL. Health and Safety Code Sections 123110; 123105; 123115; 123130; 123145

Chessick, R. D. (1977). *Intensive psychotherapy of the borderline patient*. New York: Aronson.

Choca, J. (1980). *Manual for clinical psychology practicums*. New York: Brunner/Mazel.

Cohen, R. J. (1979). *Malpractice: A guide for mental health professionals*. New York: Free Press.

Dawidoff, D. J. (1973). Some suggestions to psychiatrists for avoiding legal jeopardy. *Archives of General Psychiatry, 29,* 699-701.

Everstine, L., & Everstine, D. S. (Eds.). (1990). *Psychotherapy and the law*. New York: Grune & Stratton.

Fulero, S. M., & Wilbert, J. R. (1988). Record-keeping practice of clinical and counseling psychology: A survey of practitioners. *Professional Psychology: Research and Practice, 19,* 658-660.

George, J. C., & Sullivan, R. J. (May, 1990). Trends in malpractice claims. *The California Psychologist.*

Hall, J. E. (1988). Records for psychologists. *Register Report, 14*(3), 3-4.

Handelsman, M. M., & Gelvin, M. D. (1988). Facilitating informed consent for outpatient psychiatry: A suggested written format. *Professional Psychology: Research and Practice, 19,* 223-224.

Herlihy, B., & Sheeley, V. (1988). Counselor liability and the duty to warn: Selected cases, statutory trends, and implications for practice. *Counselor Education and Supervision, 27*(3), 203-215.

Huber, C. H., & Baruth, L. G. (1987). *Ethical, legal and professional issues in the practice of marriage and family therapy*. Columbus, OH: Merrill.

Kaplan, H. I., & Sadock, B. J. (1988). *Synopsis of psychiatry* (5th ed.). Baltimore: Williams & Wilkins.

Keith-Spiegel, P., & Koocher, G. P. (1985). *Ethics in psychology: Professional standards and cases*. New York: Random House.

Kernberg, O. F. (1975). *Borderline condition and pathological narcissism*. New York: Aronson.

Knapp, S., & VandeCreek, L. (1982). Tarasoff: Five years later. *Professional Psychology, 13,* 511-516.

Licht, M. H. (March, 1989). Ethical and legal issues: Therapy fee. *The Professional Psychologist.*

Mabe, A. R., & Rollins, S. A. (1986). The role of a code of ethical standards in counseling. *Journal of Counseling and Development, 64,* 294-297.

Mappes, D. C., Robb, G. P., & Engels, D. W. (1985). Conflicts between ethics and law in counseling and psychotherapy. *Journal of Counseling and Development, 64,* 246-252.

Miller, D. J., & Thelen, M. H. (1987). Confidentiality in psychotherapy: History, issues, and research. *Psychotherapy, 24*(4), 704-711.

Monahan, J. (Ed.). (1980). *Who is the client?* Washington, DC: American Psychological Association.

Monahan, J. (1984). The prediction of violent behavior: Toward a second generation of theory and policy. *American Journal of Psychiatry, 141,* 10-15.

National Association of Social Workers. (1996). *Code of ethics*. Silver Spring, MD: Author.

Noll, J. O., & Hanlon, M. J. (1976). Patient privacy and confidentiality at mental health centers. *American Journal of Psychiatry, 133,* 1286-1289.

Noll, J. O. (1976). The psychotherapist and informed consent. *American Journal of Psychiatry, 133,* 1451-1453.

Pope, K. S. (July-August, 1985). The suicidal client: Guidelines for assessment and treatment. *California Psychologist,* pp. 1-2.

Pope, K. S. (1988). Avoiding malpractice in diagnosis, assessment and testing. *Independent Practitioner, 8*(3), 19-25.

Pope, K. S. (Spring, 1990). A practitioner guide to confidentiality and privilege: 20 legal, ethical, and clinical pitfalls. *The Independent Practitioner, 10.*

Quinn, V. (1990). *Professional therapy never includes sex.* Sacramento, CA: State Office of Procurement.

Rachlin, S., & Schwartz, H. I. (1986). Unforeseeable liability for patients' violent acts. *Hospital and Community Psychiatry, 37,* 725-731.

Remley, T. P., Jr. (1989). Counseling records: Legal and ethical issues. In B. Herlihy & L. B. Golden (Eds.), *Ethical standards casebook* (4th ed., pp. 162-169). Alexandria, VA: American Association for Counseling and Development.

Remley, T. P., Jr. (1990). Safeguarding against ethical and legal danger points. Ann Arbor, MI: ERIC/CAPS Workshop.

Remley, T. P., Jr. (1993). "What responsibilities do I have for student counseling records?" *American Counselor, 2*(4), 32-33.

Salo, M. E., & Shumate, S. G. (1993). *Counseling minor clients* (ACA Legal Series, Vol. 4). Alexandria, VA: American Association for Counseling and Development.

Schutz, B. M. (1982). *Legal liability in psychotherapy.* San Francisco: Jossey-Bass.

Snider, P. D. (1985). The duty to warn: A potential issue of litigation for the counseling supervisor. *Counselor Education and Supervision, 25,* 66-73.

Soisson, E., VandeCreek. L., & Knapp, S. (1987). Thorough record keeping: A good defense. *Professional Psychology: Research and Practice, 18,* 498-502.

Stromberg, C. D. (March, 1989). The duty to warn or protect. *Register Report, 10*(2).

Stromberg, C. D. (July, 1990). How to respond to demands for records. *Register Report, 16*(3).

Stromberg, C. D., Haggaraty, D. L., Leibenluft, R. F., McMillian, M. H., Mishkim, B., Rubin, B. L., & Tribing, H. R. (1988). *The psychologist's legal handbook.* Washington, DC: Council for the National Register of Health Service Providers.

Strupp, H. H. (1982). The outcome of psychotherapy: A critical assessment of issues and trends. In O. J. Cavenar & H. K. H. Brodie (Eds.), *Critical problems in psychiatry* (pp. 399-421). Philadelphia: J. B. Lippincott.

Taylor, R. B. (December 11, 1988). Rape victim's diary to stay confidential, judge rules. *Los Angeles Times,* Part I, p. 52.

VandeCreek, L., & Harrar, W. (1988). The legal liability of supervisors. *Psychotherapy Bulletin, 23*(3), 13-16.

VandeCreek, L., & Knapp, S. (1984). Counselors, confidentiality, and life-endangering clients. *Counselor Education and Supervision, 24,* 51-57.

VandeCreek, L., & Knapp, S. (1993). *Tarasoff and beyond: Legal and clinical considerations in the treatment of life-endangering patients* (rev. ed.). Sarasota, FL: Professional Resource Press.

Willens, J. G., & Murray, J. R. (June, 1990). [Letter from the American Psychological Association Insurance Trust].

Wolberg, L. R. (1977). *The technique of psychotherapy.* New York: Grune & Stratton.

Woody, R. H. (1988). *Protecting your mental health practice: How to minimize legal and financial risk.* San Francisco: Jossey-Bass.

Woody, R. H. et al. (1984). *The law and the practice of human services.* San Francisco: Jossey-Bass.

Other Resources

Confidentiality of Medical Records Update

Books   Brandt, Mary
Maintenance, disclosure, and redisclosure of health information
American Health Information Management Association
919 N. Michigan Ave., Suite 1400
Chicago, IL 60611-1683
1-800-335-5535
1-708-364-1268 (fax)

Tomes, Jonathan
Healthcare records management: Disclosure and retention
Probus Publishing Co.
1-800-998-4644
1-312-868-6250 (fax)

Video   *Confidentially speaking*
An educational video showing how modern technology and office
procedures can breach patient confidentiality
Oregon Health Information Management Association
c/o MYRIAS Resources
2373 NW 185th, Suite 265
Hillsboro, OR 97124
Cost: $74.45 per video

Index

About the Authors

Mary E. Moline, Ph.D., is Professor and co-Chair of the Department of Family Psychology at Seattle Pacific University. She is a licensed marriage, family, and child counselor in California. She received her Ph.D. in marriage and family therapy from Brigham Young University and her doctorate in public health from Loma Linda University. She is a clinical member and approved supervisor of the American Association for Marriage and Family Therapists and has also taught at the graduate level for 14 years and for 2 years at the undergraduate level (California State University, Fullerton). She has coauthored a book on ethics and malpractice with Drs. Austin and Williams, published additional articles and chapters on such subjects as ethics, group, and family therapy, and has presented at local, national, and international conferences on legal and ethical issues, treatment of divorce, and cultural issues.

George T. Williams, Ed.D., is Professor of Counselor Education and Coordinator of the School Counseling Programs in the Department of Education, College of Graduate and Professional Studies at The Citadel, Charleston, South Carolina. He is former Professor and former Chair (1991-1994) of the graduate Department of Counseling at California State University, Fullerton. He is a nationally certified counselor and a licensed psychologist in California and

Minnesota and had a part-time private practice in Corona, California prior to moving to South Carolina. He has regularly taught a course titled "Professional, Ethical, and Legal Issues in Counseling." He has practiced as a certified elementary and secondary school counselor, college counselor, counselor educator, counselor supervisor, and/or psychologist in the states of Pennsylvania, Ohio, Minnesota, Louisiana, and California. He is founding editor of the *Journal of Counseling and Human Service Professions*. Within the past 15 years, he has given over 75 presentations at state, regional, and national professional conferences and has also taught over 45 different counseling and psychology courses at the undergraduate, master's, and doctoral levels. He was recipient of the Post-Secondary Counselor of the Year Award for 1986-1987 from the Louisiana School Counselors Association and, most recently, the Award for Contributions to Psychology in 1996 from the Inland Psychological Association, a chapter of the California Psychological Association. He chaired the state ethics committee for the Minnesota Association for Counseling and Development (1984-1985) and the national ethics committee for the Association for Specialists in Group Work (1987-1990). He served as state president for the Association for Counselor Education and Supervision in Minnesota (1985) and in Louisiana (1986-1987). He also served as state president for the California Association for Specialists in Group Work (1990-1993).

Kenneth M. Austin, Ph.D., is a licensed psychologist and marriage, family, and child counselor in California. He has over 38 years of experience in the mental health field. He served as Director of Clinical Services for the San Bernardino County Probation Department. In 1976, he entered full-time private practice. He was an instructor in law and ethics at Loma Linda University from 1982 to 1995 and has also taught courses at San Bernardino Valley College, University of Redlands, University of California at Riverside, and California State University, San Bernardino. He chaired the California Psychological Association Ethics Committee in 1982, 1983, and 1988. In 1984, he was presented the Silver Psi Award by the California Psychological Association. During the

1980s, he conducted workshops in law and ethics and record keeping in California, Nevada, Texas, Oregon, New Mexico, Utah, and Pennsylvania. In 1996, he conducted a mandatory continuing education workshop on record keeping for California psychologists. He is a member of the American Psychological Association, the California Psychological Association, the Inland Psychological Association, and the American Board of Forensic Examiners of which he is a Board-certified forensic examiner. Since 1984, he has served as an expert witness for the attorney general of California.